MW01248885

© 2018 Absolute Candor

Karl Staib

Bring Gratitude

All rights reserved. No part of this publication may be reproduced, stored in a retrieval system or transmitted in any form or by any means, electronic, mechanical, photocopying, recording or otherwise without the prior permission of the publisher or in accordance with the provisions of the Copyright, Designs and Patents Act 1988 or under the terms of any licence permitting limited copying issued by the Copyright Licensing Agency.

Published by Absolute Candor

Text Design by Albert Rodriguez

Cover Design by Robert Miller

A CIP record for this book is available from the Library of Congress Cataloging-in-Publication Data.

ISBN-10: 1977845495

ISBN-13: 978-1977845498

Distributed by:
Create Space
4900 LaCross Road North
Charleston, SC, 29406

Karl Staib

BRING GRATITUDE

Feel Joyful Again with Bite-Sized Mindset Practices

Absolute Candor

Bring Gratitude

Feel Joyful Again
with Bite-Sized
Mindset Practices

KARL STAIB

Preface

You're not the same person you were a year ago, a month ago, or a week ago. You're always growing. Experiences don't stop. That's life. And the very experiences that seem so hard when you're going through them are the ones you'll look back on with gratitude for how far you've come.

Admittedly, this is something simple that has taken me many years to fully understand.

As I've studied, practiced, coached and written about personal development for the past decade, I have witnessed firsthand how gratitude makes tough days more enjoyable, crazy days saner, and all experiences a lot more enlightening.

A decade ago, in quick succession, my wife, Angel, and I dealt with several significant losses and life changes, back-to-back, including losing a brother to suicide, losing a mutual best friend to cardiac arrest, financial turmoil, and more. Noticing the silver linings—the tiniest moments of gratitude—in these seemingly hopeless situations is what ultimately showed us the path forward.

Gratitude is a choice—a very positive and smart choice—at all times. The happiness of your life ultimately depends on the quality of your thoughts, through thick and thin. And this is something Karl knows a lot about, too.

Karl lost his father and it was a big spark to him writing this book. Sometimes we need a big spark to change our lives. We need things to be taken away before we fully appreciate everything we have and everything we're capable of.

Truly, Karl has been in the trenches. He understands the power of gratitude in times of heartbreak and struggle. And that's why Angel and I invited him to speak at our annual Think Better, Live Better conference two times in the past few years. His journey is one we deeply resonate with.

I know you'll find the stories in this book to be heartfelt and enlightening. We all struggle with feeling grateful at times, whether in times of personal loss, times of stress at the workplace, or times when we just want to buy something new to distract ourselves from reality. What's important is understanding the common pitfalls that get the best of us, and then shifting our daily mindset in a way that makes a lasting positive impact in our lives. It's deep work, especially when life is far from perfect, but it's worth every bit of effort you can muster!

So, right here, right now, promise yourself you will not waste your time and energy fighting against where you are. Invest your time and energy into getting to where you want to go. Let go of everything from the past that does not serve you, and just be grateful it brought you to where you are now—to this new beginning.

As you read through these stories you'll see how Karl grew stronger after his father's death, and how he used it as a springboard to improve himself and the lives around him. We all have difficulties in our lives, but it's how we use them that makes for a better, happier life.

Marc Chernoff
marcandangel.com

Five Reasons You'll Love This Book

1. You'll increase your productivity by 31%.

2. You'll learn how to fill your holidays with joy instead of stress.

3. You'll read real examples that you can use to improve your relationships.

4. You'll discover ways to adjust your mindset and let go of your anger.

5. You'll bring back the childlike delight to everyday things you don't seem to enjoy anymore.

"Gratitude unlocks the fullness of life. It turns what we have into enough, and more. It turns denial into acceptance, chaos to order, confusion to clarity. It can turn a meal into a feast, a house into a home, a stranger into a friend."

Melody Beattie

The Start

A big life event made me want to change how I dealt with my life. A small one showed me where I should begin my journey.

The major event was my father's death.

The minor event was a haircut.

Let's start with the minor one.

I was sitting, waiting for my turn, and I could feel my tenseness. When the hairdresser went to the computer and called my name, I already wanted the experience to be over.

I had so much to do, and I wondered if I really even had time to get a haircut, let alone enjoy it.

I sat down. I could feel myself getting tighter. My neck and arms started to hurt. A headache began to creep up from between my shoulder blades.

Why was I feeling this way?

Why couldn't I just relax and enjoy the haircut?

As I thought about it, I realized there were a few things causing my tension:

- » My relationship with time (I wanted to be done with the haircut and doing something else)

- » Dealing with the challenge of trying to keep a conversation going with a stranger

- » Not wanting to be confined to a chair

As the days and weeks passed, I saw this same kind of tension pop up at work, at home, everywhere.

It reminded me of my father's struggle with traffic a few months before. He was driving me to the airport after I'd flown out for my cousin's wedding. My father complained about his shins, he complained about the terrible drivers, he complained about the bad coffee he picked up . . . he complained the whole way to the airport.

His attitude kept getting worse and worse as we inched along in traffic. I felt myself pulling away from him. I didn't want to be near him, and this made me feel guilty.

I loved him so much, and I hated to see him so upset. I wished he could be at peace with something he has dealt with his whole life.

I knew I struggled with this same attitude. But I wanted to be that person people wanted to be around. I wanted to be that older person who saw the positive in everything.

A friend who worked in a retirement community once told me about an older woman there who had a great attitude even when the situation wasn't the best. She wouldn't complain about the food. She would compliment people. Everyone gravitated toward her. The staff. The other residents. Everyone.

It reminded me of a friend at work who brought gratitude to every situation. He prayed before his meal. Just a quick pause to appreciate the moment. My coworkers gravitated toward him. They wanted him to be a part of their projects. He brought such great energy and appreciation to his work.

Even uncomfortable feelings present an opportunity for gratitude. They help us take action to improve our lives. Whether we are at a job that isn't a good fit or in a dysfunctional relationship, we need those uncomfortable feelings to spur us into action. Then we can be grateful for our ability to take action and make changes in our lives.

And as we continue to take action, more emotions surface and help us to uncover more depth and joy within ourselves.

It's this circle of living that goes round and round every single day. We take an action. It causes us to feel happy, angry, sad, frustrated, excited, or nervous. How we handle these emotions determines our happiness in life and success at work. The more actions we take, the more we learn about ourselves.

After my father passed away, I felt lethargic and miserable. This book started out as journal to bring more happiness and resilience into my life. It ended up becoming a tool to help others bring the joy back into their relationships, holidays, and careers through daily gratitude. Not just through feeling grateful, but by sharing gratitude. By bringing gratitude to everyone they meet.

Gratitude starts everything

My Challenge to You

There are a lot of scientific studies about how gratitude helps people feel happier, improves their careers, and makes them more resilient.

» One study found that participants who wrote down three good things each day for a week were happier and less depressed at each of the one-month, three-month and six-month follow-ups.[1]

» Chad Burton and Laura King figured out that if people kept a journal about positive experiences, it helped increase happiness. The participants also had fewer symptoms of illness.[2]

» In another study, Richard Wiseman wanted to understand why some of us are lucky and others can't seem to catch a break. He asked volunteers to read through newspapers and count how many photos were in them. The people who considered themselves to be lucky would finish the task in mere seconds, while the unlucky ones took an average of two minutes.

I bet you are curious to why. On the second page of the newspaper was a big message that read: "Stop counting, there are 43 photos in this paper." There was also another message halfway through the paper that read "Stop counting, tell the experimenter you have seen this and win $250." The people who felt lucky were more likely to notice opportunities and take action versus the people who felt unlucky and couldn't see past their task.[3]

But why keep the feeling abstract when I can just dare you to try a little exercise and you can experience it for yourself?

Sometimes, feeling is believing.

Pull out your phone or a timer, set the timer for ten seconds, and hit start. Then close your eyes and think of as many things as you can that you are grateful for. Things like your son, daughter, wife, husband, grandmother, grandfather, dog, or cat; a sandwich, the sun, rain, your favorite nail clippers—whatever you want.

Go ahead and close your eyes and start. I'll wait.

Please try it. I guarantee it will help you.

* * *

Okay, did you do it?

How do you feel?

It's hard not to be happier when you're appreciating the wonderful things in your life. It's why I wrote this book. I wanted the benefits of gratitude to help improve my friendships and happiness, to make me more resilient and more creative. After working on this project for over a year, it's exceeded my expectations.

Gratitude is even more powerful than I realized.

I want to give you this same gift.

As you read this book, you'll see ways to apply gratitude to your everyday life. It's easy to be grateful when you are on vacation or hanging out with family or friends on a Sunday, but so much harder when you are late for a meeting and stuck in traffic.

Yet it's possible to bring gratitude to every situation you are in. It just takes a little dedication to working on your mindset.

In the following pages, I'll share the stories of my daily struggles and triumphs as I worked to understand and practice gratitude on a deeper level. At the end, you'll find a gratitude toolbox, with techniques I found helpful and exercises you can practice. If you want to take a deeper dive to bring more happiness, resilience, and success into your life, go to BringGratitude.com for more stories and tips..

1.
Just an Orange

I walked into my father's room in the ICU.

My father was hooked up to monitors and IVs.

He looked bloated, tired, and depressed. It was shocking to see the man who had always been so tough and strong looking so weak.

This man used to smash wasps with his bare hands. Wasp stings never fazed him. I thought he was the strongest father ever.

Crazy and strong.

It was my first chance to visit since he went into the hospital. I flew home because my mom wasn't sure how much longer he would live. He had been trapped by the IVs and monitors for four weeks while the doctors tried to figure out what was attacking his body, already weakened by MDS (a form of cancer).

The doctors seemed confident they would be able to help him.

As we were leaving his room to go for a walk, I asked him what he wanted us to buy for him.

He said an orange.

It caught me by surprise. When I was growing up, he drank lots of coffee and beer. He loved a good burger. I would never have guessed he would choose such a simple gift.

As my brother and I waited for the elevator, I joked with him that Dad should have asked for a Lamborghini. He gave me a weak smile. Neither of us was in a good mood.

When we came back from our walk, I handed my father the orange. He was exhausted from a raging fever, little sleep, and constant interruptions by the doctors and nurses. Yet he still managed to smile from ear to ear when he saw the orange in my hand. Tears welled up in my eyes, and I cried.

The simple joy of receiving an orange made him feel so happy. I'm sure it was because of how trapped he had been feeling. He hadn't eaten an orange in weeks.

Simple joys in daily life matter more than the big things because they occur so much more often.

We don't need big wins in life to feel happy. Small daily wins keep our mindsets strong and make it easier to appreciate the big wins.

I realized I needed to open up my gratitude to the small things.

Bust the gratitude door wide open.

2.
Overwhelmed

Numbed by what was happening.

I had been at the hospital for a few days, but my father wasn't getting any better. His MDS was preventing his white blood cells from killing off whatever was attacking his body.

His voice was fading fast.

The doctors still seemed confident they would get him back to full health. They just needed to raise his white blood cell count.

I had to fly back home.

I had just started a contract with a new company, and I had to be there. I thought for sure I would see my father when I came back to visit in a few weeks, recovering from whatever was ravaging his body.

I called him every morning on my commute to share a joke I found on the Internet. He laughed even when the joke wasn't that good. He was such a giving person in that way. I tried my best to keep it together, but I would usually cry on the phone and during the rest of my drive to work.

He was fading fast. The infection had taken hold and wasn't letting go.

He is my rock, I thought.

He laughs at all my stories. He supported me during my most difficult times. He gives me so much and now he's dying.

I realized how quickly life can fade. If I wasn't careful, I would take my last breath without opening up to what really made me happy.

I could either be grateful for everything that I experienced or angry that I was dying.

Put that way, it was an easy choice. It's easier to change a habit when you can see clearly what will happen if you don't.

I wanted to feel grateful for what life I had left.

3.
Simple Water

The pain in my stomach subsided.

I finally felt normal. A little tired from a rough night's sleep.

Then I thought about how we needed milk and I should make a run to the store. If I didn't run to the store now, we wouldn't have milk for cereal. And if we didn't have milk, the morning with the kids could go sideways. That's when it all hit the emotional fan.

My worries almost took over. It's amazing how one little worry can create a domino effect, setting off a thousand more.

Then I thought about how lucky I was to feel normal again. I didn't feel any stomach pain. I didn't feel perfect, but I felt so much better than I did the day before. I had energy again.

Striving to feel perfect is a losing game.

We don't have a worry, problem, or pain maybe about 1 percent of our lives. It's a great feeling, so we try grasping for this feeling all the time.

It's why travel is so exhilarating, why we love new gadgets. I realized I was easily distracted by new things. Trying new food, visiting museums, hiking in nature, buying a new phone, etc. I didn't worry as much when I had these to focus on. But when my head hit my pillow, my worries wouldn't turn off.

I didn't appreciate simple things as much as I should because I was always striving for something new. It was time to change this mindset.

A cup of coffee in my living room could be just as amazing as it was in a Parisian café. I just had to be willing to appreciate the nuances that I typically ignored.

If I could find gratitude in the everyday things, then I know I could be happier. Everyday things happen so much more often than a vacation or buying a new gadget. There are just more opportunities to enjoy daily things than new things.

Even something as simple as a glass of water.

When I look at things from a fresh perspective, the water isn't just water that I can drink. It's water that nourishes me. Whether it's the water's temperature or the taste, I can find a way to savor it.

This kind of appreciation can make any moment feel interesting.

4.

Unexpected Lessons

My stomach was a mess.

I knew I was getting older, but this was ridiculous.

For the past few months, I'd had an off-again, on-again queasy feeling, with heartburn on top of it all.

Then I had a conversation with a friend. She told me that her daughter had stomach issues too. She had an ulcer just like me. She also told me that her daughter had always been very anxious.

For years I'd tried to push away my feelings of anxiety, but with this conversation, I realized I couldn't ignore them any longer. I'd struggled with anxiety for a while now. The only thing that kept me sane was my yoga and meditation practice—at least a few minutes at the end of each day.

The problem was, I couldn't wait until the end of the day to feel relaxed.

So I decided to put more focus on watching my body's cues. The main symptom that I kept experiencing was tightness in my chest, which I assumed was due to heartburn. Turned out, it was due to heartburn, but it was triggered by my chest-breathing.

When I was feeling tense, I would breathe very shallowly and into my chest. On this day, I decided that I would focus on breathing into my belly. That was my main focus for the whole day.

My brilliant friend Mike uses the term "theming." He's a productivity expert. He themes his days, weeks, months, and years.

I applied this idea to my mindset. By making my whole day about breathing, I was able to dig deep enough to really see a difference.

My muscles relaxed. My stomach relaxed. My mind was more relaxed. I felt ten times better.

I was amazed by the way focusing on my breathing could improve my perspective. Breathing into my stomach made me more aware of how tense I'd been. This awareness helped me stay much more relaxed throughout the day. It also cut down on my heartburn.

Breathing deeply, I was grateful for what the moment offered, not what it didn't.

5.
Monsters

I snapped upright in my bed, suddenly awake.

My heart was pounding.

In my dream, I'd been running from a big monster that I couldn't see. It was very dark. I could hear its deep breathing behind me. I felt like I was seven years old again. I kept tripping on small objects on the floor, and the monster kept up with me at every turn.

I turned a corner, and my dad was there to catch me. Even now, when my conscious mind knew he was in the hospital, some part of me felt he was there to help protect me.

He said, "Don't worry. Everything will be okay."

The dream felt so real.

It was weird to think he might not make it out of the hospital. The doctors couldn't figure out how to help him fight off the infection or whatever was inside of him. I felt that my dream was trying to help me process my father's illness.

I got up and went to the bathroom.

When I came back, I lay down, but I was wide awake.

I tossed and turned.

I looked at my phone to check the time. I had two more hours to sleep before I had to get up for work.

I tried counting sheep and I was still wide awake.

I tried pretending I was in a warm bath, floating on the surface.

I tried putting on my headphones and listening to sounds of rain.

Nothing.

Just wide awake.

I decided to go and read a book. A book that I was familiar with, so I could relax. I read one of my favorites, Turn Your Mind into an Ally.

I read a page about staying in the present moment. It's one that I must have read a dozen times, but it always grounds me. One that I really needed that night.

As I continued to read, I realized that I was lucky to have this book, a glass of water, and a few more minutes before I had to get ready for work.

6.
Kiss on the Neck

We had an argument about our holiday gift budget.

It wasn't a major fight, just a husband and wife getting on each other's nerves.

Later that night, my wife was cooking dinner and I noticed the French toast wasn't that crispy. I asked if she would turn up the heat on the pan so the French toast would cook faster.

She snapped, "I already did."

"Whoa! I was just asking."

She doesn't like it when I try to give tips on cooking, especially when she is already mad at me. I could see her point. I don't like people telling me how to cook when I'm in the middle of cooking either.

Still, I was a little frustrated because she snapped at me when I was just trying to help. She was frustrated because I was butting in when she didn't want me to.

Instead of holding onto these feelings, I'd been working on just letting them go. And also engaging with the person I'd upset. Not letting things fester and build.

I decided against a typical apology. Sometimes a typical apology can seem demanding if the other person is still mad. They'll reluctantly say, "It's okay" or "It's not a big deal," when to them it is a big deal.

Instead, I asked the kids if they wanted a "flying kiss" and they said yes. So I zoomed in like an airplane and gave them both kisses.

Then I looked at my wife, and I asked her if she wanted a "flying kiss." Of course she said yes. I swooped in and gave her a kiss on the neck.

I saw the tension release from her shoulders. Then she gave me a quick smile, and we were good again.

7.
Bloated

I woke up at 3:00 a.m.

My stomach ached. I rolled out of bed. The gas buildup in my stomach made me feel stretchy and bloated.

I walked around the house to calm my stomach. I finally fell back asleep, but I woke up again at 5:00 a.m. feeling even worse. I just couldn't stay asleep.

When I finally got up, I knew it was going to be a rough day. Then I realized I was setting myself up for a lousy day.

So instead of labeling it "rough," I decided to label it "challenging." I thought, What would be a good question to help set up my day so it will be a bit more enjoyable?

I'd been practicing on asking better questions to reframe the way I look at things, and this was a perfect opportunity.

I decided on:

What will be the most interesting part of not having enough sleep?

Throughout the day, I observed how I felt as I worked. I noticed I was lightheaded. I also noticed I was more prone to eating chocolate than usual. And maybe the most important change was in how I dealt with others. I was much more likely to be impatient and curt with people.

This awareness allowed me not to feed into my impatience, but instead to relax with it.

Instead of putting people down in my own head, I tried to appreciate people for who they were in that moment.

My question helped shift my focus from my lack of sleep to the way that I behaved as a result. It helped turn my day from one of internal complaining to one of curiosity.

Maybe it was curiosity that killed the cat, but at least he had an interesting life while it lasted.

8.
Tough Battery

The corner of my finger bled.

It was my fault.

The battery in the keypad garage opener had been failing for a while. I'd known I needed to replace it. My garage opener does not like to operate in the cold. Very much like myself. I'd procrastinated for over a week, and now I was locked out.

I called my wife, and she pressed the garage opener inside the garage and let me in the house. It wasn't a big deal, but I felt frustrated because I shouldn't have procrastinated.

I found a new battery and went to replace the dead battery. I needed a screwdriver to take off the plastic casing. As I tried to pry open the casing, I held the screwdriver, flashlight, and battery in one hand. My gloves were getting in the way, so I took them off and held them too. I slipped and the screwdriver cut my thumb. It bled. I dropped everything and growled.

I'd been rushing through the process because I was cold. I should have set up myself for success by placing everything I didn't need to hold on the ground. I also should have slowed down. Replacing a battery isn't difficult. It just requires more focus than I was willing to give it in that moment.

After I cut myself, I took a breath and felt grateful for the lesson to slow down a bit. The blood on my thumb showed me that I could have avoided this pain if I had been willing to plan out my task a little better.

I apologized to my thumb and gave it a kiss.

This made me laugh.

I picked up my screwdriver, leaving the rest of my things on the ground. I got the case off and replaced the battery.

It's a great feeling when I learn from my mistakes. It doesn't happen as often as it should, but when it does, it sure feels good.

9.
Grasping for Perfect

I dropped my son off at school and headed to an offsite meeting.

As I pulled out of the school parking lot, I tried to merge into a turn lane. The driver there wouldn't let me in. A minute later, my phone GPS app crashed. I threw my hands in the air.

"Oh my God, I can't catch a break! Com'on, why are you testing me so much this morning?"

My tension was building with every mile.

I stopped at a red light. Because my car was stopped, the music seemed very loud.

It irritated me. I felt like hitting my radio.

I turned it off, took a deep breath, and looked around. Seeking something, anything, to appreciate about the traffic. The variety of cars to look at. From red to yellow and big to small. The intriguing curves and shapes the designers created.

The beautiful trees.

The soft seats in my car.

There was so much to appreciate.

I could feel my stomach muscles release.

The red light had forced me to pause, encouraging me to notice my tension.

My blood was boiling because some stressed-out commuter wouldn't allow me into the turn lane. I could let this reaction continue, or I could use this moment in my anger to release my tension.

I appreciated these feelings of tension. They showed me that I was overreacting. This pause helped me slow down and relax just a bit. Just enough to exhale and take a breath in. I could feel my jaw was tight. I released my tense muscles. I then took a moment to appreciate my awareness.

I exhaled again and breathed in this calmer me.

I said to myself:

Pause

Exhale

Breathe

Release

Appreciate

I repeated those five words.

Pause

Exhale

Breathe

Release

Appreciate

P.E.B.R.A.

I decided that would be my new acronym for when I was feeling stressed out. If I used it enough, maybe I'd remember it. I repeated it in my mind until I got to work.

When I stopped grasping for a better situation, I was able to enjoy my current situation again, which made it better.

"Give yourself a gift of five minutes of contemplation in awe of everything you see around you. Go outside and turn your attention to the many miracles around you. This five-minute-a-day regimen of appreciation and gratitude will help you to focus your life in awe."

Wayne Dyer

10.
Last Words

My father's last words to me were ones that he struggled with most of his life.

"I love you."

He could never say this to me when I was growing up.

It became a joke in our family.

I would say, "I love you."

He would say, "Me too."

I know he loved me, but he was a tough German who didn't show much emotion.

When he said "I love you" that day over the phone, I pulled my car over and broke down crying.

It was his final gift to me. I'll cherish it until I die.

Later that night, when I pulled into the driveway and walked inside, I walked up to my wife and my sons Gavin and Erik, and told them that I loved them.

I explained that their Opa died and told them that I was going to miss him so much. It still feels surreal as I write this, but I'm so grateful that I could learn from him how to be strong—and even, in his last days, how to be a little more vulnerable.

11.
Floating Leaf

I felt out of place.

I called out sick to take some time to process my father's death.

All I felt like doing was streaming movies, avoiding my pain.

Instead of giving in to this temptation, I decided to go for a walk.

My father loved walks. He breathed in the trees. It calmed him.

I often listen to interviews on my walks. But this time, I wanted to just be with my thoughts. As my thoughts swirled around missing my father, I started going into a dark place, feeling sorry for myself. I worried about my relationship with my boss. I worried about my oldest son's anxiety issues. I worried about my own anxiety issues.

Then I looked down and saw a leaf swept up by the wind. It broke my negative trance.

The leaf fluttered up, then floated gently back down to the ground. I didn't feel a gust of wind. Maybe because I was so lost in my thoughts. Or maybe that leaf stirring was God—or the universe, or whatever you want to call it—helping me to focus on something, anything, besides my dark thoughts.

Instead of going back to my dark place, I latched on to this breadcrumb of gratitude. I moved my focus from the leaf to the trees to the beams of sunlight that burst through to the grass. Then to a conversation I'd had with my coworker about the value of a creative outlet.

I started to enjoy my walk.

12.
Ho Hum

It was a bleak day.

Rainy.

Regular.

Everything felt ho hum. Very normal.

The travel bug grabbed me and started thrashing me around. I felt desperate for adventure. I looked at flights and hotel rooms on my phone during lunch. Every place I wanted to go was very expensive.

We couldn't afford it.

I went to work the next day with a sour attitude. I didn't feel like being there.

As I was walking into work, I stumbled and dropped my thermos. The metal clanked on the ground. CLANK, CLANK, CLANK. It echoed around the office.

My coffee didn't spill because of the great thermos my wife bought me.

Instead of picking it up and pretending like I never dropped it, I just stood over it for a second to soak in the moment. That clank was a noise I hadn't heard in a while. I felt a little embarrassed, but not so much I felt like hiding. I took this time to learn from the situation.

I didn't need to travel to have a new experience. I just needed to appreciate and enjoy what I could experience. So, I went into work looking to have conversations with new people. I talked with a guy at work who'd written a book on fine dining restaurants. I hadn't even known he was an author.

He told me about a few restaurants to try out. I told my wife that we were going to have a sitter watch the kids on Saturday while we went out to a nice restaurant he'd recommended.

My sour attitude had changed into an interested one. I ordered the half chicken on top of seasoned veggies and was blown away by how good it was.

It made my week.

13.
Lightning Shot

I stood up, and lightning shot through my back and down my left leg.

I had to sit back down. The pain was like a thousand little needles jabbing my skin at once.

I had been sitting for too long.

I knew keeping my blood flowing to my muscles was very important. But sometimes I got too caught up in my work and forgot, and then this happened.

I've noticed my brain works that exact same way. When I stop challenging it, it stops finding creative solutions.

It's easier to just stay put (physically and mentally), but that doesn't mean it's better for me.

So how do I keep moving when it's easier not to?

It's about finding gratitude in the challenge. If I can turn any situation into a growth experience, I'll be able to appreciate any moment.

When that feeling of lightning shot down my leg, it felt like a warning shot. If I kept on this path of not moving around throughout the day, I would continue to experience pain like this.

I knew I needed to improve my habits. I felt so lucky that I received this challenge to improve my health and grow. I could choose to see it as an opportunity instead of something to complain about to my wife.

I started with a simple change: using a smaller glass to drink water. When the glass was empty, I would have to get up and get more. This little change started a domino effect of more movement at work and at home. Now I also use a standing desk, and this encourages me to move around more because I'm already up and ready to go.

Coming up with little triggers to get me moving—things like that smaller glass of water and standing desk—was exactly what I needed. I haven't felt those lightning bolts down my leg since.

14.
Old Traps

It was a Thursday, late in the day.

I was hungry.

At work, my idea to improve the website page was shot down.

I was disheartened. Another meeting and I wasn't valued.

At least that's how it felt.

Then my coworker Clarissa said, "I know you're disheartened, Karl. I would be too. I appreciate that you are trying to create a better experience for our customers. Your hard work matters."

Those words were exactly what I needed at the time.

Sometimes I forget that no job is perfect.

No team is perfect.

No one is perfect.

I also forget how lucky I am to have a great job.

Lately I'd been falling back into old habits, complaining about my job. Thinking that people didn't know how hard I worked. Griping that it was hard to get people to listen to me because there were so many layers of red tape.

The reality is that I'm lucky to have so many talented and caring people around me, people who are trying to improve the company and build stronger relationships with me. I get to laugh at work on a daily basis. Someone usually brings in tacos or donuts at least once a week. I also get to work in an air-conditioned building and take paid time off when I'm sick. The perks are plentiful.

I'm lucky to have an imperfect job that challenges me to grow.

Remembering to appreciate the people that I work with and all the good things that come along with my job can help me keep things in perspective.

15.
3:00 A.M. Wake Up

"I just threw up," I heard in my dreams.

I opened my eyes. It was pitch black in our bedroom. I thought, Who said that?

I waited.

"I just threw up," my son said again.

He had come into our room, looking for my wife and me to help him.

I was tired from working late and just wanted to stay snuggled underneath the covers.

I need to help my son. The thought was brief, just popped into my head.

There was this quick moment of feeling grateful for the ability to help him. It spurred me to get up and put my feet on the ground.

My wife and I got up. My son had thrown up all over his bed. It smelled terrible.

I helped my son get undressed and cleaned up. I got him a glass of water and stood with him while he brushed his teeth. My wife changed the sheets, threw them in the washing machine, and put new sheets on his bed.

He got back in bed, laid his head down, and closed his eyes.

"Poor guy," my wife whispered to me.

"Yep. He's a tough little dude," I replied.

She nodded.

If someone had asked me fifteen years ago if I would ever be grateful for waking up at 3:00 a.m. because someone threw up, I would have confidently said no.

Fast forward to today, and I can confidently say yes. I felt grateful to be able to help my son. To make a rough night a little easier for him. Helping him was way more important than my own sleep.

16.
Spreading Ashes

With my wife, my mom, and my brother, I headed into the woods behind my childhood home.

We were there to spread my father's ashes.

My father's death changed me.

I lost a best friend and my number one supporter. He believed I could be a great writer when everyone else rolled their eyes at me.

I will always remember how he felt when I hugged his soft body in the hospital bed. He wasn't the strong German man I grew up with.

He was fragile like the rest of us.

As we walked up the hill, we crunched through the leaves and picked trees that we thought my dad would like to help grow. We spread ashes under the most beautiful trees on the family property.

We wanted him to live on through his trees.

Man, did he love his trees. He refused to cut any down, even when our shaded pool struggled to warm up in the northeast summers.

He passed many of his values on to me, and I am so grateful for every moment that I had with him.

I now have the tools to live a great life because he helped me build my internal toolbox.

He always said, "You'll never get this moment back. Just enjoy it for what it is and don't expect it to be any different."

My father will always live on in me, my brother, my mother, my sons, and his trees.

Thanks, Pops!

17.
Small Deaths

I heard a loud honk.

I snapped out of it and looked up to see that the light was green. I pressed on the pedal to zoom through the intersection.

I didn't know how long the light had been green. I'd been out of it since my father passed. I'd never mourned at this level before.

Processing my father's death had thrown me for a loop.

I missed him.

A lot.

The world felt a little different. Coffee didn't taste as good. A walk on a trail was about my dad's death instead of about enjoying nature.

As I drove, I appreciated this time to process everything in my life. I felt like I was becoming a different man. I remembered how, in my mid-twenties, I flipped my car because I was driving drunk. How that moment changed me. Sent me into a depression.

There are daily small deaths within us. These small deaths open us up to becoming happier and more grateful people.

We have choices that we make every single day. Eat an apple instead of a donut. Take a walk instead of plopping on the couch. Work on projects we care about instead of reading articles on our phones. The more we let old habits die, the more we can do things that help us grow happier.

When I gave up drinking, it was because I'd realized it did me more harm than good. I just didn't enjoy it anymore. It's a small part of me that died.

When something dies, we need to process it. To mourn, in a sense.

Sometimes that's mourning the death of a loved one; other times, it's mourning old habits that we no longer need.

Taking the time to mourn that drinking, reckless part of me allowed me to move on and become a happier me. Now, as I mourned my father's death, I was learning so much about myself.

I'd gotten so angry over small issues because I didn't process my feelings very well. I'd been afraid to embrace these feelings. I'd ignored them, just like my dad used to ignore his feelings.

We build happiness through appreciating small moments, things as simple as peeling an orange. Through asking, "How can I enjoy this situation?" or "How can I learn from this situation?" instead of focusing on just getting through it or complaining about it.

When we practice enjoying the process of peeling an orange, we're laying the groundwork for handling bigger issues.

Mourning my father's death was helping me slow down and understand why I acted the way I did and how I could continue to push outside my comfort zone for the growth that I sought. It sounds weird, but in a way, I was learning to be grateful for my father's death. He taught me so much, and day by day, I saw a little more clearly how to use this knowledge to create the life that I wanted.

He wanted me to be my own man. To learn from him and do something great.

It reminds me of a great quote by Sir Isaac Newton:

"If I have seen further it is by standing on the shoulders of Giants."

Thanks again, Pops! You are still teaching me even after your death.

18.
Red Light

The light turned from yellow to red, and I barely moved ten feet.

I was still stuck waiting for the light to turn green. I hoped I could make it through the next one.

I was late for a very important meeting. I had to present to my boss and other managers the experience that I wanted to change on our website.

The meeting couldn't start without me.

I slammed my fist on my steering wheel. Screamed as loud as I could.

Now my fist and throat hurt.

My level of anger surprised me.

Then I asked myself a simple question:

"What choices do I have to improve this situation?"

I realized I did have choices.

I could slam on the gas and bust right through the red light. I could quit my job and give up my career. I could pray for aliens to come and beam me aboard their ship. Or I could text my boss and let him know that I was going to be a few minutes late.

I chose the last option.

With that simple text, I reduced my stress by 90 percent.

You have choices in every situation you are in. It's up to you to be creative and think of the best way to handle the situation.

19.
I'm Lucky Because . . .

The pain shot up my leg and into my neck.

One quick ankle twist, and I fell to the ground in agony.

My dog didn't even realize that I'd dropped the leash and was lying on the sidewalk.

I yelled out, "Hey!" and she stopped and sat down without even turning around.

I got mad. "Hey, stupid!"

She turned around and saw me on the ground. She came running back to me.

I was taking my frustration out on her. This made me feel even worse.

I sat up on the curb and assessed the damage. Later that night, my ankle blew up to twice its normal size. I needed to stay off it for a long while.

That was a few months ago, and now my ankle is completely healed. A few years ago, I probably would have just forgotten about the twisted ankle and kept going about my life.

The more grateful me takes the time to appreciate a simple walk from my car into work without any pain. Sometimes it takes some pain to appreciate how good I have it. To remember how lucky I am to have a healthy body.

When my ankle doesn't hurt, it's a glorious day.

Right now, I'm balancing on one leg as I type this, because I can.

A good memory is an important part of tapping into gratitude. Remembering past pain can open our eyes to the joy of its absence. Daily living is full of distractions. It's good to take a moment every now and again to focus on how lucky we truly are to walk down the street and be able to enjoy everything around us.

20.
Stand-up

I stood there looking at the floor. The gray and black patterns in the rug seemed more interesting than the meeting.

We call these meetings "stand-up" because we stand and give our updates about our projects. For this one, I was feeling insecure and tired.

I didn't give my usual enthusiastic update.

After the meeting, a coworker came up to me and asked if I was okay. I told him I was a little tired, but otherwise I was feeling okay. Then I really thought about it. Not only was I tired, but I was feeling scared about not being able to deliver on my end of the project. This had never occurred to me before that moment.

Later that day, I told Matt (my closest friend at work) how I was feeling. It was a big relief. He told me he often felt similar in the middle of a tough project. He suggested I bring it up in the next meeting. It's why we have the meetings, he told me.

I'd been afraid to embrace my insecurities because I didn't want to show any weakness, but in hiding from these emotions I only multiplied my insecurities, showing everybody how I really felt with my body language and voice. The one thing I wanted to hide was on full display for everyone to see.

The next day we had stand-up again, and this time I talked about what I was struggling to accomplish. Someone offered to help.

A simple, honest confession was a huge relief.

We all worked together and were able to meet the deadline.

I believe I was only able to do this because of my friend Matt. I truly appreciated him taking the time to talk with me. He asked simple questions like "What is the worst that could happen?" and "Do you want to keep feeling this way?" He opened me up so I could explain what was going on inside my own head. I would've kept ignoring my feelings if it weren't for him.

The next time I'm feeling a little insecure, I plan to notice it, embrace it, and acknowledge it to the people around me. Then just see what happens.

21.
Success

I'd finally arrived.

I had a really good job that allowed us to remodel our bathroom, but I felt like something was missing.

I felt empty.

I wanted to be grateful, but I saw a friend's post on Facebook: he'd just given a keynote talk at a big conference. I felt this jealous pain ripple throughout my body.

How could I be jealous?

I had a healthy family, a great job, and money to do fun stuff.

After I read his post, I realized I wanted more.

Instead of feeding my jealousy monster, I came back to gratitude. I thanked God for my health, my family, my freedom, my comfortable shoes, my creativity, and my ability to think positive thoughts.

I started to calm down and feel better.

I also realized that I wanted to help more people. My jealousy was trying to teach me a valuable lesson. I wasn't doing enough to make a difference. Jealousy can be a good kick in the pants. I felt inspired to write more and speak more about gratitude. It's one of the reasons this book is in your hands.

I'm grateful for my talented friend whose Facebook post inspired me to do more with my career. He spurred me to take a little more action instead of feeling sorry for myself.

22.
How You Compliment Matters

"I'm so lucky to have Mark on my team," my coworker Amy told me. "His attention to detail is off the charts."

I also like Mark. He's a good guy.

Amy's compliment made me feel good for Mark.

Surprisingly, Amy's compliment also made me feel good about Amy. When she shared her gratitude for Mark, I appreciated her a bit more. I wanted to help her more than I already was, so she would be grateful for me too.

After our conversation, I did a little research. I wanted to know why Amy's compliment made me feel good about her.

I found out that when someone gives a genuine compliment to a teammate, like Amy did, then we tend to respect the person who gave it. This is a great way to show gratitude because it creates a win-win, benefiting everyone involved.

Who knew that bringing gratitude to work could help your career?

23.
Giggling Softly

He giggled softly.

I looked over at my two-year-old and asked him what so funny. He looked at me and said my shirt was tickling his foot.

I didn't even realize that his foot was right next to me.

Something as simple as my shirt helped my son become more aware of his foot. That was a cool surprise.

It's so easy to stay entwined with our thoughts. Sometimes I forget the simple joys of my sensations.

As I was first writing this, I was in my chair. I stopped, paused, to feel my body.

My neck felt tight, and my legs felt tired. I started scanning other parts of my body. I scanned both feet touching the ground, my ears, my forehead—which was tense. I relaxed it. Relaxed my shoulders. And noticed the air going in and out of my body.

I felt happier than I had all day. I took the time to just be in the moment, and it felt great.

24.
From Ear to Ear

The skin around her eyes crinkled.

Her lips creased into a smile.

I smiled back, then sipped my tea.

My tea had never tasted so good.

I was lucky to have this talented person helping me grow my side business. I didn't have a lot of time, and I needed all the help I could get.

She thought about how I could improve my business not only from a marketing perspective, but also from a sales and customer experience standpoint. She suggested that I focus my business on customer engagement instead of surveys.

She nailed it.

She explained why she thought the way she did and how each part of her approach would affect my business.

I was very impressed.

I complimented her on a well thought-out proposal. I explained to her exactly what I liked.

She was over the moon with delight, beaming from ear to ear. I made her day because I acknowledged how hard she had worked on the proposal that she gave me.

I have to remember that I need to show gratitude for people's hard work more often than I already do, especially if they exceed my expectations. They deserve appreciation.

I've noticed that when I give specific details about the aspects of someone's work I really enjoy, it builds their confidence and encourages them to keep doing top-notch work. It's funny how long it's taken me to figure this out. Complimenting others doesn't come naturally to me. My father was not one to give praise or gratitude very easily, and that has influenced me.

Whether you are at work, out with friends, or at home with the kids, try giving just one genuine compliment, and watch the reaction. It may make more of a difference than you expect.

And the more you practice, the better you'll get at it.

25.
Choose Laughter

The man stopped his car right in front of me and started turning around.

I had to slam on my brakes. "What are you doing?!" I screamed.

I was on a mission. I needed gas, and this guy was turning around right in front of me. My only option was to wait for him.

After he turned around, he drove right by me without a courtesy wave. How, I wondered, could he be so rude?

Then I realized he might be embarrassed. He'd made a mistake, and I was making him feel worse about it. How could he look me in the eye?

It reminded me of my conversation with my friend Rob after I shared with him that I was writing a book on gratitude. He told me that when he gets treated rudely during his commute, he chooses laughter.

I started to laugh. A gentle laugh at first, then I let it grow.

I laughed at how angry I was over something that caused me only a ten-second delay. I laughed at my embarrassment. I laughed at a tough conversation with a coworker that I had last week. I laughed at my frustration with my kids not picking up their toys. My laughter increased, and I started laughing because I was enjoying myself.

It felt strange at first, but then I felt good. I actually felt great. It was the release I needed from the tension that had been building up over the last few days.

I felt so lucky for my friend Rob.

The next time I'm having a tough moment in traffic, I'm just going to laugh it off. I'm going to start laughing, and even if I feel embarrassed, I'm going to give in to the laughter.

26.
Stepping Away

"Let's take a walk," I told my coworker.

He looked up at me, nodded, and said, "I could use a walk."

His shoulders relaxed. He stood up from his chair. He pointed toward the hallway and asked me, "Is that the way you want to go?"

We had hit a mental wall. We didn't know which way to go with the project. I thought a change of scenery would help us.

We walked around the office, discussing our plans for the next project. Then he had a great idea. One that turned everything on its head. He suggested adding a slider to an important landing page on our site to gauge how interested our visitors were in our underperforming product.

It fit with what we needed to do perfectly. We needed to do a better job engaging our visitors instead of selling them on something they might not need.

When we got back to my coworker's desk, he looked at me and said, "Thank you so much. I'm so glad we took this walk."

By stepping away from our work, we were able to figure out a solution. A simple break in routine allowed him to step back and see the problem in a different way.

27.
Freedom at Every Turn

I'd been invited to an important meeting.

We were going to review some of the faults in the designs my team and I had created.

I was leery at first, but once we started talking, I could see that we were looking for solutions, not blaming people.

It ended up being a really good meeting full of great ideas.

A few years ago, I wouldn't have been able to enjoy that meeting. I would've been silently screaming to get out of the room. Most of it would have been due to fear. Fear of people judging me and thinking that I was stupid.

Now, I was grateful for the opportunity to be there and voice my opinion, no matter what people thought. I felt freer in that moment than I had in years.

Free to be me.

Freedom doesn't come from being in a wide, open space.

Freedom comes from mindset.

There is no switch that you can turn on or off to make these feelings possible. It comes from watching, learning, and letting go. Just letting the moment be as it is. Not trying to change the situation.

As I left the meeting, I felt this joy that I'd never experienced before that moment. A sense of freedom that I think I'd been afraid of enjoying before that day. I savored it for as long as it lasted.

28.
The Final Judgment

The truth was . . .

I was afraid.

When I was in my twenties and early thirties, I was afraid to put all my energy into projects and have them fail. I didn't want to be judged, so I stuck to meeting minimum requirements. I kept my jobs, but I never wowed anyone.

Recently I delivered on a tough project, and the person leading the project said, "This is great, Karl. You went above and beyond. Thank you."

It made me feel good, but it didn't define how I felt about the project. If he had told me that my work wasn't what he expected, I still would've been proud of myself because I put a lot of effort and hard work into the project.

One secret to satisfaction at work is appreciating the work we do at every step of a project. From research to completion.

I've learned that I'm the final judge of how I think each project turned out.

This time, I already knew about all the hard work I put in. I already appreciated it.

All the person leading the project did was put a little cherry on top.

29.
Captain of My Thoughts

It was dark, and I was lying in my warm bed.

My first thought was:

Why do I have to get out of bed?

I didn't want to take off my covers.

Then I realized that my first thought was not helping me take action. So I asked myself:

What would be a better way to look at the situation?

That led to another question:

What do I enjoy about taking off my warm covers?

I thought about the cool air rushing to meet my legs, about placing my feet on the ground, and about going to take a shower. I saw a lot of potential joy in the next action I needed to take.

I smiled.

Last Thanksgiving, I remember having a similar thought:
Why can't we stay home this year?

I worried about making small talk and not being able to watch the football game without being distracted. The truth is, I don't even remember the score of the football game, and I always seem to enjoy the small talk once I'm there.

Step by step, I'm learning to become the captain of my thoughts, instead of letting them dictate how I feel.

30.
An Ocean of Food

I was looking into a kitchen with food on every flat surface.

It should have been hard not to be grateful.

The thing was, I didn't feel very grateful. I'd just had an awkward conversation with my cousin.

Earlier in the year, he'd been in the hospital. He'd almost died.

This was the first time I'd seen him since his health scare occurred.

I didn't know what to say. I was at a loss for words.

Can you be grateful for almost dying?

There seems to be a fork in the road when people have a near-death experience. Either everything gets better or everything becomes a bigger struggle.

My cousin didn't seem any happier, but some people don't show their happiness in waves of positive emotions. Some people just accept and move on.

I tried to bring my mindset back to one of gratitude, but I couldn't take my mind away from the thought of my father's death. I wanted to feed into my pessimistic thoughts about my father's death. My own death as well. This path looked so enticing. It had the comfort of familiarity. I'd been down it so many times before.

I started listing all the things I was grateful for, but it was a struggle.

I felt like I was forcing gratitude, faking it, so I took a short walk. I went outside. Saw the fog of my breath float away and dissipate. I looked up at the leafless trees and let out all the air in my lungs, then took a giant breath in. The joy came, then quickly faded.

I walked some more and wrapped my coat tighter about me. Such a great coat.

The gratitude ember flickered brighter. I took another deep breath. I was starting to feel a little better.

I thought about my father's influence over me as I turned from a boy into a man. My father will always be with me. He wasn't perfect, but he challenged me to be a better person, father, and friend.

At first, that conversation with my cousin seemed like something negative, but with the power of gratitude, it turned into something that took me on this little mental journey that I didn't expect. A journey that challenged me to open up to parts of my life that I was ignoring.

It's good to think about things like death. It doesn't have to be negative or overwhelming. It can be cathartic and freeing if we can find the gratitude in our darker thoughts. They can help us grow stronger and happier.

My father's greatest lesson was:

If you are going to take the time to do something, then do it well.

I realized I was half-assing gratitude.

No more fooling around. If I wanted my life to be filled with gratitude, I had to practice it in every situation that I was in, every day.

My father's death had made me stronger. More resilient. I appreciated his love. The love he gave me mattered more than I ever realized. He was ready to move on, and so was I.

31.
This Is It

"This is my life." My friend hung his head.

"Yep," I replied.

"I just wish . . ."

He went on to rattle off his complaints. From a broken dryer to a terrible boss.

I knew the feeling.

Sometimes even when you know your life is great, it just doesn't feel that way. My friend had a great wife, he was healthy, his kids were healthy, and he had amazing friends. He wasn't happy at work, but that didn't mean his whole life was in shambles.

"I've been there," I said, "but what if you spun this situation on its head?

What are five things you are grateful for right now?"

"I really don't want to . . ."

"Just humor me for a minute."

"Okay." He thought about it. "Ahh . . . I'm grateful for . . . my daughter, my son, and . . . my home, my wife, Netflix, and oh . . . my camera."

"That's good," I said. "How would you feel if tomorrow you got out your camera and took pictures of all those things?"

"Even Netflix?" He smirked.

"Sure, if you want, but at least take pictures of your daughter, your son, your wife, and your home, and see how it makes you feel."

"Yeah, I like that idea," he said. "Thanks, man! I think that will help."

32.
The Thank-You Card

Going over a friend's house for dinner is a fun part of the holidays, but it can be stressful too.

It's not just showing up and eating. You have to make small talk, dress nice, bring some food with you, and teach your kids the value of good manners.

To be honest, it freaks me out sometimes.

As we were getting ready to leave the house, Gavin (my seven-year-old) asked why we were bringing dessert. We explained that we wanted to contribute to the meal and show our friends our appreciation for inviting us over for dinner.

My son asked, "What can I give them?"

My son is full of surprises. He'd never wanted to give anything to our friends when we went over for dinner before.

I suggested he draw them a picture. He liked the idea, so he ran to his room and grabbed his markers. I got out a piece of paper.

"So, what do you want to draw them?"

"How about a thank-you monster?"

He drew a monster with six outstretched arms and six mouths. His arms and mouths were ready to give hugs and eat all of the food.

It was a great card.

When we arrived, our friends opened the door, and Gavin jumped up and handed them the card. Our friends smiled and gave my son a hug.

My son brought gratitude with him to our friends' home.

33.
Thanksgiving Meal

I love Thanksgiving, but sometimes it's just too much to handle.

It feels like it needs to be perfect. The food, the clothes, my attitude.

It can just be another meal.

A meal with really good food, family, American football.

This year, it was my turn to give grace.

I gave a short one. I didn't want to steal the show.

"I'm grateful for all of you.

"You make me think, laugh, cry, and grow.

"I feel so lucky that I love to eat turkey and stuffing and salad and it's all right here before me.

"I remember when I used to look at my father piling on the salad. When I was a kid, I used to think he was crazy. What am I thinking, of course he was crazy. When he offered me some salad, I would scrunch my face and say, 'No thank you.' He always used to say, in his German accent, 'You don't know what you are missing' and of course he'd pile on an extra scoop to show you how great this salad was. I'm going to miss him.

"To Baba. Cheers!"

34.
The Power of Gratitude

I'm working harder now than I ever have in my life.

I'm doing it for two reasons. One reason is for my family and the other is for the feeling I get when I do great work with my team.

I've noticed the simple statement "Thank you so much for all your hard work" matters enormously to me.

I enjoy managing multiple projects at once. It challenges me and pushes me outside my comfort zone.

The more I can manage, the more people I can help. Making sure I don't overdo it and run myself ragged is important, so I've been working on taking breaks and setting limits.

I used to jump headfirst into new projects and fizzle out because of the lack of positive feedback. Now I get that positive feedback from more than one source. My career, my hobbies, my side business, my side projects, etc. I'm getting more praise now than ever before.

It spurs me to stay focused and to do great work.

When the gratitude stops, my motivation dies with it. The money helps, but people showing me appreciation is what truly drives me to improve.

It's a good reminder, because I know that I can fall back into bad habits. I need to give my coworkers gratitude when they deserve it, so they can feel the power of gratitude too.

"Gratitude is the healthiest of all human emotions. The more you express gratitude for what you have, the more likely you will have even more to express gratitude for."

Zig Ziglar

35.
Traveling Home

The alarm went off at 4:00 a.m.

It was pitch dark.

I tried to wake the kids up. They were rocks. Unable to move. My wife was double-checking the suitcases to make sure we had everything.

Traveling back home to visit my family for the winter holidays was stressful. It wasn't just the stress of traveling, but also who would be there.

One of my friends and I'd had an argument a few months ago, and I really didn't feel like seeing him. But I'd have to, because we had the same circle of friends.

This added stress kicked up my anxiety about going home. I worried about how he'd react to me.

I played it out in my head a few times, planning what I'd say. Then I noticed that I wasn't bringing any gratitude to the situation. Even with all my gratitude practice, I was still falling back into old habits.

I went to the bathroom to brush my teeth. I started listing all the things I was grateful for about the upcoming trip:

» Watching my kids look out the airplane window

» Seeing my mom

» Giving my brother a hug

» Meeting my cousin's baby for the first time

» Reading a new Winston Churchill biography

» Going out to eat with my friends

» Enjoying the Christmas lights around my mom's neighborhood

» Taking a walk with my sons at a nearby park

» Savoring the Christmas turkey and mashed potatoes

I thought again about meeting my friend, and decided to apologize for my stubbornness. Now I could add:

» Apologizing to my friend and patching things up.

This list went on, but it had already made a big difference in my attitude. I saw the potential beauty in my trip instead of focusing on the most difficult parts of it.

36.
My Aging Body

» Back pain

» Depression

» Neck pain

» Cancer

» Varicose veins

» Abdominal pain

» Headaches

» Knee pain

» Hip pain

- » Shoulder pain

- » Ulcer

- » Sore throat

- » Stomach virus

- » Walking pneumonia

- » Infections

This is all just in the past seven years.

We all deal with pain every single day, from hunger to tired muscles. And there are different ways to handle it.

How you handle pain will be a huge factor in your happiness.

Pain is much easier for me to handle now than it was ten years ago. I've gained wisdom through the pain in my past, and I'm grateful for that. It makes me stronger.

I try to use pain as a tool for growth. I'm not always successful, but I believe it's something to strive for.

For example, if I stub my toe on the coffee table . . . do I get mad?

I've noticed that my level of anger is determined by my mood.

If I'm in a good mood, I'll laugh at the pain.

If I'm in a bad mood, then I'll swear or hit a cushion, letting the pain linger.

An occasional swear word doesn't bother me. It's just a gauge of where my mindset is at when the pain rushes through my body.

By opening up to this little sliver of appreciation, I'm able to understand a little more about myself. This is where the deep internal growth occurs. If I ignore it, then I'll keep handling similar situations the same way, which gets me the same results.

37.
Five Deep Breaths

Stop everything.

Stop Everything!

STOP EVERYTHING!

I had been feeling very overwhelmed. The holidays were getting to me. I felt like I was juggling three jobs. One was getting ready for the upcoming holidays, another was my career, and the third was my side business. It wasn't easy trying to stay on top of it all.

This seemed to happen every year.

I found myself talking so fast that I was starting in the middle of my story and not giving the proper context for the situation. That's always a good sign that I feel stressed out.

My friend said, "Slow down. Stop worrying. Just take a breath."

So that's what I did.

I walked outside, about twenty feet from the building's entrance, and took five very deep and long breaths.

I felt so much better.

I was surprised that I needed somebody else to tell me to do this. Sometimes we need an outside reminder to stop ourselves from feeding into every overwhelming emotion.

I felt lucky that I had a friend to show me that I needed to pause. That I could be grateful. That I could slow down and take five breaths. That I didn't need to be rushing to finish the current task so I could get to the next one.

We can take five very long breaths anytime we want. Slow down long enough to let the gratitude in.

38.
A Little Switch

I was in a very important meeting.

I heard a buzz from my phone.

I picked up my phone to check the text message I'd just received.

I felt like everyone was watching me. I dug in deeper and told myself I had a right to check my phone.

Of course I had a right to check my phone, but that didn't make it the best choice in the moment.

I should've been more focused. I was in a critical meeting that required my attention.

On my drive home that night, I replayed the situation over and over in my head. I was tougher on myself than I should've been. I lost sleep that night because I was worried about the impression I made.

When we make a mistake, we can beat ourselves up about it, or just learn from it and let it go. But even when we want to let things go, sometimes that's easier said than done.

At lunch the next day, I caught myself still thinking back on that meeting and worrying about what people thought of my phone etiquette.

Then I thought a little bit more and realized how much I care about my job and the people I work with.

That's a good thing.

A really good thing.

My real mistake was not that I acknowledged my lack of self-control and was mad at myself, but that I wasn't willing to let it go and forgive myself.

After realizing this, I felt so much better. That thought was like a little switch inside of me. I was able to let my mistake go once I had learned something from it.

In the future, I thought, I'll try not to let myself get too carried away with checking my phone, so I can show people how much I care about being there. Otherwise, they may think I don't care as much as I do.

39.
It's How You Feel

We were stuck.

Cars lined up on the freeway as far as the eye could see. Holiday traffic is always difficult to appreciate.

I started thinking that it would take us an extra hour to get home. The kids would need to stop to pee or to get a bite to eat. I could feel my neck and my shoulders tensing up.

It was because I'd been more mindful lately that I was able to notice this so quickly. I'd been much more aware of my thoughts since starting a conscious gratitude practice, but difficult situations still stressed me out.

A few months ago, I read a book about mindfulness. The author kept talking about how he used to think about potential problems instead of enjoying the present moment.

He thought about how the airplane staff might not have his favorite drink, because that's what happened last time. He thought about how his doctor appointment had been canceled, and now he'd have to reschedule it. He thought about how his stomach was slightly upset and maybe he should take some antacids, but he didn't have any so he would have to buy them at the airport and pay too much for them.

It was a good read, but he missed an important point.

The problem isn't just that we think about too many things. Life is about how we handle these thoughts. We can't always stop them from occurring, so what about looking at how we can use our thoughts as a springboard to an improved perspective?

For example, I might think:

My stomach is a little upset and I have to buy medicine to help me feel better. I hope this goes away before tomorrow.

Or

My doctor appointment was canceled. When is my next appointment going to be? I'm probably going to have to wait two more months.

When I have those thoughts, I can handle them from a place of gratitude:

My stomach is a little upset and I have enough money to buy antacids to help me feel better.

Or

My doctor appointment was canceled, so now I can finish writing my report. Or maybe do something fun like making a trip to my favorite store, walking in the park, or spending some extra time with my family.

The key is finding ways to be aware of these thoughts. When we accept them and focus on the potential positive in the situation, we can feel grateful instead of feeling stressed out. It's all too easy to worry and allow ourselves to get all worked up over something that isn't really a big deal.

Next time you see your thoughts start causing you stress, try embracing them. How can you use them to see the positive in your situation?

This week, I found myself in a traffic jam coming out of a packed parking lot. I decided to see if I could enjoy five things about being stuck in traffic.

1. The man in the car behind me had a 1920s style hat on, which I thought was cool.

2. A tree in the parking lot only had one lone leaf clinging on.

3. I made a "nanny nanny boo boo" face at the kid sitting in the back seat of the car stuck beside me. He smiled and did it back to me.

4. I took three deep breaths and enjoyed them.

5. I put on my favorite album and jammed out the rest of the way out of the parking lot.

Success!

40.
Gurgling

My stomach gurgled after dinner.

I felt a bit queasy, but I didn't feel like throwing up.

I wasn't sure what to do.

I felt like I needed a quick fix.

I didn't feel like eating, lying down, or doing something active.

I've dealt with stomach issues all my life. A few years ago, I gave up ice cream, followed by all dairy foods. Next was red meat, then some grains, and finally foods with a high concentration of sugar. I've tried eliminating all kinds of foods, and there have always still been stomach issues for me to deal with.

That evening, I felt like I was playing the waiting game. Waiting for my stomach to feel better, so I could enjoy life again.

Then I had a thought. What would happen if I leaned into these feelings instead of just wishing they would go away?

I sat down on the floor and relaxed as I scanned my body from my feet all the way up to my head.

It's interesting how sometimes a similar lesson presents itself to me time and time again, but I can't seem to learn it. I knew I was a bit thickheaded, but this needed to sink in sooner rather than later. I shouldn't be afraid of my upset stomach. I needed to do a better job of watching and learning from my body.

I also knew I shouldn't beat myself up too much about this issue. It's a common struggle, one many of us share.

Donuts and beer are good examples. These are not healthy options. But that doesn't mean we never choose them.

I knew that my stomach problems usually happened when I was feeling stressed and overwhelmed. They'd start out subtle and get more and more intense the more I ignored them. I kept trying to power through.

I needed to be more aware of how I handled situations at work, so I could be more relaxed and able to function well. During the last project I was working on, I didn't ask for help when I needed it, and I let my tension build. Fatigue took over, and I ended up getting sick and having to call out of work for a day to recover.

The more we appreciate and watch how our feelings affect our health, the more often we can recognize when we need to take time to relax before we become overwhelmed.

41.
Tears

Tears were streaming down my coworker's cheeks.

She was completely overwhelmed.

"I can't do it all. I just can't keep up. My boss wants it done before the end of the year. I was planning on taking off between Christmas and New Year's, and there is no way I can do that with all my work. I'm going to have to cancel all my plans."

"You don't have to keep up with everything," I said. "That's what I'm here for. How can I help?"

"You can't help me."

"Just try me."

She explained how she had too many projects and her director kept dumping more projects on her.

She was wrong about one thing.

I could help.

I asked her to give me one of her projects. She explained that she couldn't. That she needed someone who could help her write code.

That's not a skill I possess.

I got up, found a senior developer on another team, and asked if she knew anyone who could help. She was able to send someone over later that day.

The guy was amazing. He helped my coworker finish the three projects by the end of the week. She made her deadline. She was so happy.

"Thank you so much for listening and helping. I was this close to quitting." She held up her thumb and index finger, a raisin-width apart.

"Really?"

"Yes, you saved my job. You saved me."

42.
Missed Deadline

I made a huge mistake.

I thought I could finish the project by the end of the week. I was so wrong.

I didn't realize how many people I had to depend on to get the project done. I stayed late. I ran around like a chicken with my head cut off, asking for answers so I could keep moving forward. I brought in a couple other people to help at the last minute, but it wasn't enough.

I missed the deadline. The next window to get this project finished wouldn't be for another three weeks because of the dependency on other teams. We would potentially lose thousands, maybe even millions, of dollars.

I cried. I called out sick. Just didn't want to be anywhere near work.

And I blamed myself.

I called a friend from work and complained about my situation. He asked me a question: "Was anyone else willing to take on this project?"

"No."

"That's right," he said. "You were the only one willing to stick your neck out there trying to get this project done. Instead of beating yourself up, you should be congratulating yourself for trying so hard. Just because it didn't work out the way you hoped, it doesn't mean it's a failure."

Then he asked me another great question.

"What did you learn from this experience?"

I laughed and said, "Nothing," which I knew wasn't true.

As I thought about it, I realized that if I'd been more compassionate with myself, I would have known that I couldn't do it all by myself. I should've brought in other people to help me sooner. It's funny how not that long ago, I could see how my coworker needed to ask for help when she was in a similar situation, yet here I was, unwilling to admit I needed help. I realized that this was a skill I needed to work on to improve my happiness and my career.

In retrospect, I was so glad I got caught in this situation. It showed me that I had a lot of internal work to do. I resolved to focus on asking for help sooner. I knew that practicing this in everyday situations would help me build up my strength to do it when I needed help the most, so I didn't get caught in a similar situation in the future.

43.
Keeping It Weird

Christmas music blasting in my car.

A warmer-than-usual winter day.

Stopped at a red light.

I rolled down my window.

Put my hands to my mouth and made duck calls into the setting sun.

Feeling good.

44.
Great Questions

"Jingle Bells" was softly playing in the background.

My friend and I were sipping coffee.

She said, "Can you say that again?"

I said it again:

"A good question always trumps a good answer."

She replied, "Yes!"

As we were sitting there, I realized something important. In most conversations, I was focused on grasping for greatness. I wanted the conversation to be memorable.

This one was easy and enjoyable, because I was appreciating our conversation and not wanting it to be different. I wasn't trying to be smart and funny. I was just listening and building on my friend's ideas.

Once I started to appreciate others for who they were and not who I wanted them to be, I began to enjoy conversations so much more.

I noticed little details in my friend's face. Like the slight wrinkles at the corners of her eyes. The inflection in her voice. As I focused on what I appreciated about her, the conversation became even better.

I said, "I'm curious, why did you like that statement so much?"

She told me she liked it because a great question allows the other person to shine. And if you can allow the other person to shine, they feel good about themselves. Isn't that what great relationships do for people?

Yes!

45.
My Fever Spiked

My nose was running.

My fever spiked.

This flu wouldn't allow me out of bed.

I thought, Why hasn't modern medicine figured out how to solve the flu?

Another small-minded question.

Two steps forward and two steps back in my gratitude journey.

It's hard to ask good questions when I'm not feeling well. But this discipline of gratitude matters even more when I'm sick.

I chuckled, then coughed.

The human body is a marvelous virus killer. It's not perfect. My father's body couldn't fight off whatever virus or infection was inside of him. But my body was working hard to fight this virus off, and it was going to succeed. It was doing the best it could with what I gave it.

I knew good food would help me heal. I decided to go and eat an orange. And it was a damn good orange.

Modern medicine has done so much for our society. Too often, we forget about how far we've come and don't take the time to appreciate it.

While sniffling and coughing, I took a moment to thank my body for working so hard to fight off this flu. I also took the time to think about how lucky I was that I had medicine that helped me sleep at night.

So much goodness to focus on—even when my head felt like I had a fishbowl over it.

46.
Spilled Milk

The milk went all the way down my back and all over the floor.

I should have seen it coming, but I didn't. It's easy to forget how important awareness is until you miss something important.

I'd picked up my two-year-old son when he had a cup full of milk.

Bad idea.

My first reaction was to be mad at my son, but the reality was that it was my fault.

I laughed at my lack of awareness. I made a mental note not to pick up any child who is holding a cup of milk.

You would think that I would just know this and not have to make a mental note not to do it again. I guess I just learn at a different speed than others.

Next, I turned into the milk monster and roared. My son laughed. I put him down and was about to chase after him, but I thought better of it when I realized the possibility of getting more milk all over the floor.

I roared again and pretended to drink the milk going down my back with my very long giraffe tongue.

A small part of me appreciated that I could actually enjoy having cold milk spilled down my back. My mind is more flexible than it was a few years ago. I'm able to enjoy so many different kinds of situations, even when I act like a blockhead.

It's amazing how far I've come.

47.
Money Issues

"I'm not sure I can afford Christmas this year. It always seems like I need to top myself from the previous year. My credit card debt is only going up. It's a difficult cycle that I can't seem to break. I need to make a change," my friend told me.

I knew the feeling.

I struggled with money in my younger days. Always wanting the latest gadget. Always wanting to impress people with the gifts that I gave. Living paycheck to paycheck.

Then I decided to try an experiment.

I would spend much less. I would get everyone a small gift, but I would make cards to go along with each of them. As I did this more and more, I realized that people talked more about my handmade cards with my simple sixth-grade drawings and lists of why I was grateful for them than they talked about my gifts.

That's what they remembered the most about my gifts.

My brother still talks about the cool cards I made him. He never talks about any of the gifts. I don't make as many cards as I used to, but it's time I got back to it.

48.
Labels

A big meeting was coming up.

My hands were sweating. My stomach gurgled at the sight of food.

I was nervous, to put it mildly. My anxiety was ticking up, and I felt like hiding.

Then I remembered a conversation with an old friend.

"Your attitude about your feelings will dictate your response," my friend had told me.

You can run from your feelings, or you can appreciate how they make your life interesting.

The more intense the feelings, the more interesting life becomes.

I enjoy feeling life deeply, but sometimes, feelings can become overwhelming. Emotional balance comes from finding the right mindset.

In the time before that meeting, I had a choice. I could run away and throw in the towel, or I could find a perspective that would help me cope with my feelings.

So instead of labeling my feelings as "nervous," I chose the word "excited." It was my theme for the meeting. I began to think of different ways that I was excited, and how that excitement was affecting me.

I was excited to present to the whole group.

I was excited to share my ideas with them.

I was excited to hear their thoughts on my ideas.

My excitement was picking up my heartbeat, helping me focus, and making my hands and armpits sweat.

My excitement was energizing me.

By relabeling my nervous energy as excitement and thinking through the ways I could apply it, I was able to reframe how I was viewing my situation.

Now I was leaning much more toward feeling excited. I still felt the nervousness inside of me, but it was tolerable. My presentation was now a challenge that I could take on—and kick butt while doing it.

49.
Pouring Hot Water
into My Tea Mug

As I was pouring hot water over my tea bag, I quietly whispered, "Thank you."

It just popped out of me.

At first, I wondered who I was thanking.

Then it occurred to me.

I was thanking God.

I've poured tea for myself over a thousand times and never said thank you.

I used to only check in with God when I needed help or for something that felt important like a Thanksgiving meal.

Never ever would I thank God over something so simple as tea.

It was early morning, and my family was all still in bed.

It felt very calming.

Working on gratitude has helped strengthen my connection to God.

This is an unexpected perk. I was raised Christian—Lutheran, to be precise. I never realized how much had sunk in when I was young.

I don't attend church, but I do believe in a higher power. Something that gave me this life and this earth to enjoy. Eventually my life as I now know it will disappear, and knowing that helps me enjoy it just a bit more.

My father didn't believe in God, and I think this played a role in his struggle with being thankful. He expected things to always be as they were, and when he started fading, he didn't have anything to help him with his worries and pain.

It was cool to see how much God mattered to me. It helped ground me in joy.

After that morning with the tea, I decided to try silently thanking others. Thanking people for letting me help them or thanking a stranger sitting in a coffee shop because seeing them made me feel good.

The ability to give a silent "thank you" to others is a gift for me too.

It's another form of prayer.

50.
Eating Pie

I wanted just a little more.

I wasn't sure why.

I'd had two big slices of pumpkin pie, but I wasn't satisfied.

This confused me. Usually I'm fine with just one slice of pie, but today even the second slice didn't make me happy.

I relaxed and thought about what could be causing my unease.

Work had been stressful lately, and I noticed my thoughts gravitating back to it even when I wanted to enjoy a family meal.

Eating pie distracted me from my worries. I was so caught up in my own thoughts that as I finished each piece of pie, I realized I had barely tasted it.

Eating mindfully is a skill I still need a lot of practice on.

When I'm worried, I usually eat too fast, causing my stomach to feel upset. When I'm grateful for each bite and take my time, I don't overeat and I feel so much better.

I stopped myself from taking a third piece of pie and decided to drink some water instead. I filled a glass and took my time drinking it, feeling the water go down my throat. With each sip, I started to relax.

My tension eased up enough so I could enjoy being around my family again, and even enjoy the simple sensation of being in my own body.

51.
Christmas Morning

As the wrapping flew off the gifts, I felt this unease.

I wasn't enjoying myself.

I couldn't stop thinking about my father. We were in the home he'd built with his own hands. I knew he shouldn't be with us because it was his time to move on, but I couldn't help feeling sad.

My wife handed me a gift, and when I opened it, my unhappiness kicked up a notch. It wasn't the portable speaker I'd had on my list. I'd wanted an Amazon Echo—a voice-controlled speaker that I could use to play music from Prime, Apple Music, Spotify, and other streaming services.

This speaker had to be connected through my phone to play music.

I looked at my wife and asked, "They didn't have the speaker I wanted at the store?"

She frowned.

I had upset her.

I felt even worse. I wasn't being grateful. I wished I could take my words back.

She said she'd researched speakers and this speaker had the best ratings out there.

I thanked her, but I couldn't hide my disappointment in the gift and in myself.

It wasn't my wife's fault that I was missing my father and was grumpy. I'd acted like a spoiled brat, not getting the speaker that I wanted.

My gratitude practice had hit a low point.

I vowed to try harder.

I needed to practice letting go of wanting my father to be with us and to allow each moment to be as beautiful as it was, even with my father absent.

I went to grab a cookie from the table. The cookie reminded me of my coworker who pauses for a prayer before he eats his meals. What a great way to pause and slow down, so he's more likely to be thankful and savor his food.

I decided to pause before I opened my next present, so I had time to silently thank the person before I opened it. I needed to practice receiving something wonderful from someone. Silently giving thanks gave me time to warm up to the idea of receiving the gift—and to consider how lucky I was to receive any gift at all.

52.
Basics

I sat in my chair and waited for an answer.

I didn't know what the next steps for my project would be. It looked like no one else knew my next steps either.

I could feel my anxiety rising.

I knew this because I always breathe shallow when I'm worried. I was breathing into my chest instead of my stomach. This doesn't help me make smart choices. It makes me tighten up.

I blurted out, "Doesn't anyone know what needs to happen next?"

The room was stunned.

I was stunned by my actions.

It was right then that I knew I needed to exhale and take a deep breath.

I apologized.

Then I steered us back on track. "So what is the part of the website that most customers are confused by?"

We proceeded to look at the most important parts of what we needed to fix, then categorized them by importance. We all began to feel more relaxed.

I've been working with my breathing for a few years. It's a recurring lesson in my life that is finally taking hold.

Lately I've been talking with my friends about good breathing. I give them an example. I ask them to exhale and take a breath in. About nine out of ten of them breathe into their chests.

Give it a try.

Exhale.

Now breathe in.

What part of your body expands?

If your chest expands before your stomach, you aren't breathing as well as you could be.

If your belly expands first, great! You can keep building on this skill to stay calm in a stressful situation.

Good breathing helps with anxiety, stress, digestion, and energy. If you can learn to take most of your breaths into your abdomen, you'll be much more relaxed and have more sustained energy throughout the day.

53.
So Frustrated

My two-year-old did not want to wear any of the shorts I'd picked out.

I was already late for work. I didn't have any early meetings, so I wasn't too stressed, but I didn't want this struggle to go on for hours.

My son would agree to a pair of shorts. He would put them on and then throw a fit, complete with tears and thrashing on the floor.

I was so frustrated.

I still needed to grab a snack for work, so I took a break and went to the kitchen to look for something I could bring with me. Instead of complaining to myself, I decided to thank God for the situation I was in. I was lucky to have such a strong-willed and healthy son who was forming his own personality.

Taking this break and reframing things allowed me to reset my mindset.

I walked back to my son's room. He was sitting on the floor with a shirt in his lap. He'd found a different shirt that he wanted to wear.

"Can I wear this monster shirt?"

It had a smiling monster with shark teeth on the front. It was a cool shirt.

I felt thankful that I didn't force him to wear something that wouldn't have made him happy.

I asked him to pick out his shorts as well, and he found something right away. He was back on track. We headed out the door.

My new goal for the week is to thank God for the situation that I'm in whenever I'm frustrated, so it gives me a chance to pause and reset my perspective.

54.
Thank Everything

Thank you, bed covers, for your warmth.

Thank you, cool air on my legs as I take off the covers, because you help me wake up.

Thank you, feet, for taking me to the sink to brush my teeth.

Thank you, designer, for designing a great toothbrush.

Thank you, Nikki, for allowing me to kiss your soft neck in the morning.

Thank you, kids, for helping me practice letting go of my frustration.

You get the point.

A week ago, I'd set a goal of thanking God for all my frustrating moments.

Today, I focused on silently thanking everything that I could. It helped when I thought through why I was thankful for each thing. It made it more concrete.

At times, it was hard. I lost focus for long stretches, but whenever I came back to this "thank everything" practice, I got an energy boost and felt more relaxed.

As I thanked my pillow and closed my eyes, I also noticed that I'd had one of the best days that I'd had in a very long time.

55.
Grasping for
a Better Moment

My son looked at me.

"Dad, it's your turn."

I was checking my phone because my client had just messaged me.

"Hold on, I—"

I caught myself before I could finish telling him the rest of my thought.

"I'm sorry," I said to him.

I'm addicted to my phone, just like I'm addicted to my thoughts. Of course, my phone helps me in many ways, but that doesn't mean I should let it dictate my life.

A few weeks ago, I'd caught myself checking my phone in an important meeting. I'd resolved to be better about it, but I felt like this habit was only getting worse.

I got up, put my phone in the kitchen, and sat back down with my son.

I hadn't been with my son 100 percent. I'd been grasping for what I believed would be a better moment. I couldn't have been more wrong.

As we played, I noticed myself feeling agitated when my son took a long time with his turn.

I wanted to get up and grab my phone so I didn't have to wait. I could at least be productive.

This internal rationalization to allow myself to use my phone was an interesting one. I knew I checked my phone when I shouldn't every now and again (that meeting last month came to mind), but I'd never thought of myself as someone who had a bad habit of checking my phone too often.

I saw that I'd been wrong.

I had to let go of wanting to check my phone every two minutes. To enjoy this moment with my son. The best way to do this was to acknowledge my irritation and be grateful that this situation was showing me a nuance in my personality that I needed to face.

56.
The Power of Gratitude

"Down there!"

My two-year-old son pointed to a toy underneath the table.

I was tired after a long day, and I did not feel like leaning down underneath the table and grabbing the little red car that had fallen.

Then a quick thought flashed through my mind: I'm lucky to play with toys at the table with my son.

It spurred me to bend down and pick up the toy.

He smiled and said in his two-year-old voice, "Tank you."

His gratitude made the moment memorable.

57.
Stuck in Traffic

Stuck at a red light for the fourth cycle.

The lights were on a short timer and every time my light turned green, cars were blocking the intersection, so my lane couldn't get through the light.

I looked around for a place to turn off. No luck.

It was probably going to take another four cycles for me to get through.

I growled in anger. I hit my steering wheel.

I was pissed off.

Getting frustrated in traffic was still a recurring theme in my life. Sometimes I'd find a way to find gratitude at a red light, and it would work for a week or so, but then it would peter out, and I'd get frustrated and impatient. It was time to try something new. Again.

I looked around and saw a young guy dancing in his car as he waited at the light.

He was better at this than me. I could learn from him. He was having a grand old time.

I pulled out my phone and put on one of my favorite songs by Of Monsters and Men. I sang along at the top of my lungs while I danced in my seat. I was lucky to have so much great music at my fingertips.

And I car-danced through the rest of the traffic jam.

58.
Miss the Pain

I put my head in my hands.

I didn't know what else to say.

My oldest son refused to clean his room until he found his little toy T. rex.

Every sentence I said to get him to focus on cleaning his room instead of finding his toy made him dig his heels in even more.

I decided it was my turn to be more flexible.

"Okay. We'll set the timer for ten minutes. If we find the toy or the timer goes off, then you have to clean your room. Deal?"

He nodded his head yes.

It's funny how someone's most difficult personality traits can help you grow.

You usually don't remember that easy project at work. You remember the hard ones that you had to drag to the finish line.

The most difficult times are the most memorable, and oftentimes the most shared. When you raise a smart and curious kid, you have to expect that they will challenge you.

I expect it now, and it's easier to handle.

He has recalibrated our relationship.

It's these stories that my wife and I talk about all the time. It's become a part of our family DNA.

These difficult moments were often painful at the time, but usually because I made them more difficult than they had to be.

As we've grown together, I've asked him to be more flexible, but the reality is that he was and is still teaching me to be flexible with him and with my life. I thank my lucky stars I've had—and have—such a stubborn boy to raise.

The timer went off, and we still hadn't found the toy. He was okay with picking up his toys. As we picked up his toys and put them away, we found the T. rex in his closet. I felt like Super Dad. It's too bad we don't find more lost toys when cleaning his room.

59.
Another New Year

The pops in the distance woke me up.

The fireworks were going full tilt.

It was midnight, and my neighborhood celebrated with style.

I had been in bed for over an hour already. Glad I felt comfortable just lying in bed, not afraid that I was missing something.

That's the nice part about getting older.

You don't need to go all out because you're scared that you aren't living life to the fullest. Every day is a day filled with hugs, kisses, good food, hard work, yoga, meditation, bike rides, piano lessons, clipping toenails, or drinking a tea with a friend.

It was great to see fireworks in Rome, redwoods in San Francisco, and the Mona Lisa at the Louvre. It was great riding the train through the Alps in Switzerland. But those experiences are just a small part of my joy. Every ordinary day brings fireworks of joy that I'm lucky to experience.

60.
Gotta Believe

I remember when I was young. Maybe six or seven years old. I would hear the door open from the basement, and I would run to the top of the stairs. My dad would be unlacing his boots, look up, smile, and say, "Hey, buddy!"

He always gave me a big smile.

It's why I loved making him laugh. His eyes would squint and the skin to the side of his eyes would crinkle up.

He owned his own electrical contracting business. He believed in his work.

It filled him up.

Work can be such a beautiful thing. A meaningful project lifts our spirits, and this influences the people around us. Big ideas are fun and make us feel alive.

When we stop taking action on our big ideas, it's often because we're afraid the final product won't be as good as we would like it to be.

Expectations are the number one killer of our happiness.

It's okay if the current big idea doesn't meet our expectations, because we will learn from it and make our next projects that much better. I've had three failed businesses, and this is my fifth book. None of the others has been a big success. What I've learned from them is that I'm not scared of failure any longer.

That's why I'm succeeding.

I'm only getting smarter and stronger with each project. With each project, I meet amazing people. Each person helps me grow. Even if a project I work on doesn't succeed in a monetary sense, it helps me understand my work on a deeper level.

That's the amazing opportunity we all have—let's take advantage of it in every way possible.

61.
Teamwork

I was working on too many projects at once.

One project in particular was taking a lot of time. As I was knee-deep in this difficult project, I got a request to make some changes to another project.

I was overwhelmed.

One of my coworkers could see my frustration and asked if everything was okay. I almost said yes, but then I caught myself.

"I could really use your help. I'm not sure what I should do here."

I pointed to my computer screen.

He looked at it. "We had a similar problem last year."

"Can you help me?" I asked.

"Sure. I'm a little slow right now," he said.

I explained what needed to be done and went back to my other difficult project. He came back to me a few hours later with all the required changes.

I felt so lucky to have him on my team.

Knowing you can count on others can be a big boost to your career. Don't be afraid to ask for help when you need it. People will probably be happy to help, and you'll be happy for the stress relief

62.
Get Granular

I sat down in my car and felt myself sink into the cloth seat.

It was oddly gratifying.

I'd just finished a hard day at work, and I was mentally exhausted.

That seat made me so happy.

Instead of rushing to turn on my engine, I took a breath and just enjoyed the quiet moment.

It's relatively easy to be grateful for a good friend or a great sandwich, but when I started taking the time to dig a little deeper, I began to uncover some real gratitude gems. Like appreciating a stoplight because it helps keep order on the road, instead of complaining that it's slowing me down or keeping me from getting home.

It was funny how much I enjoyed thanking everything, but would nonetheless slowly drop out of the habit over time. Then, when I was mentally wiped out, I'd remember and start again.

I started my car and thanked it for starting up without any issues. As I backed out of my parking space, I paused to look at the building where I worked. It was beautiful. It allowed me to do great work and earn money for my family.

As I drove home with this granular gratitude, I felt a weight lifting off of my neck.

You've probably heard some phrase along the lines of:

> When you try to become a master of something, you deepen your appreciation for it.

It's why people often enjoy watching sports they used to play. They realize how hard it is to play at the level of a pro.

Granular gratitude was the next step of my journey, and it turned out to be an amazing tool.

By paying attention to the little details, we began to change how we view our day-to-day experiences. Everything becomes a little more vibrant and interesting.

63.
Thanksgiving Flashback

I scooped a good bit of stuffing and plopped it on my plate.

I wasn't sure why I'd made stuffing with dinner. It was the middle of the winter, and I guess I just wanted some stuffing.

It was the store-bought kind. If it was a few years ago, I would have focused on the fact that it wasn't made fresh, but this evening I was focused on enjoying the food.

It hit the spot.

I slowed down and savored every bite. I noticed my wife and my oldest son were doing the same thing.

I felt this deep sense of gratitude. Maybe because stuffing gives me flashbacks of Thanksgiving.

Gratitude supports my ability to savor something. They are intertwined.

I slowed down and really let the moment sink in for all it was worth.

I can savor a sip of water.

Savor the struggles of writing this book.

Savor a hug from my wife.

Savor a walk into my kitchen.

Savor a deep breath in.

Savor the moment after a long walk when my body is all sweaty.

Every moment can be amazing with the right mindset.

64.
Playing Blocks
with My Sons

Sitting on the floor with my two sons felt amazing.

We were eating pancakes and playing with blocks on a Sunday morning. Gavin created towers, and his little brother, Erik, knocked them down.

I noticed a slight inclination to check my phone, but I didn't. I was learning. I wanted to be in this moment 100 percent.

"Hey, Dad, what should I build next?" Gavin asked.

"How about a lighthouse and a boat in the water?"

"Okay."

He started building. Erik put another small pancake in his mouth and waited to knock down the newest structure his older brother was building for him.

"I'm done. What do you think?" Gavin asked.

"That's awesome," I told him.

Erik perked up. Looked at his brother for approval.

"Yeah, Erik, you can knock it down."

Erik walked over, swung his arm, and the blocks went flying. We all cheered.

It was a magical hour that I truly enjoyed. I felt so glad that I hadn't hopped on my phone and distracted myself.

Every moment is magical when we are willing to give our full attention to it.

65.
Every Moment
is Magical

Walking through my living room, I stepped directly on a Lego block.

It jammed into my heel. I fell to the floor.

Is this moment magical?

It's a tough question to ask when you're sitting on the floor, taking deep breaths and holding your bruised heel.

I was mad.

My gut reaction was to yell for my boys to come pick up their toys.

I'd done this in the past and regretted it, so I took three deep breaths.

I looked around, and I actually felt grateful for a messy house. I remembered when I was single and alone, and how I wished for a wife and family in my life. Now I had it.

When I put it in this context, I knew I was a lucky man.

Every moment is magical when you know that it will fade away. It's your moment and no one else's. It's up to you to enjoy it for all it's worth.

I calmly called for my boys to come and pick up the Legos they'd left in the middle of the floor.

66.
The Beauty of Prayer

I was talking with a coworker who was having trouble in his marriage. His wife was struggling with depression, and he didn't know how to support her.

"She is just unresponsive," he told me. "I come home and the kids are crying and she has this dazed look on her face."

As he was telling me his story, I noticed this subtle happiness come over me.

I ignored it at first. Then a second wave of happiness came, a little stronger.

I felt ashamed. I wanted to hide my joy.

How could I be happy when someone's marriage was struggling?

I didn't hate my coworker. I liked him a lot. He was a good and caring guy.

Then I got it. His pain made me realize that I was lucky to have a wife who not only was strong and caring, but also wasn't struggling with depression. I was also glad I wasn't struggling with depression anymore myself.

This didn't make me feel any better. I cringe as I write this. I don't want to be that type of guy.

But these were the feelings creeping into my consciousness.

I'm far from perfect. I accept this, but internal growth is important. I want to be a better person. I want to be a person who hopes for other people's success.

When we encounter feelings we're ashamed of, we can either try to bury them or we can acknowledge them and use them as a way to grow.

I created a plan. Not just to feel gratitude for this friendship, but to spur myself to improve how I view similar situations.

What does a golfer or pianist do when he wants to get better?

He practices.

I had to practice being compassionate for others, so I went back to my Christian roots. I prayed for my friend and his family. I prayed that his wife would get help and feel better. I prayed for him and his kids. I also let my friend know that I was available if he ever wanted to talk with someone.

Prayer can also help with jealousy.

Recently, a coworker told a small group of us how much he was paid. It was significantly more than I was. I felt some pangs of jealousy. Instead of feeding these jealous thoughts, I first focused on appreciating him, and then I prayed for his continual success.

The beauty of prayer has no bounds. It's a silent gift we can give to others.

I know I'll probably feel happiness at someone else's expense in the near future, but I look forward to the challenge of improving my attitude toward other people, in both their failures and their successes.

And I pray that others will do the same for me.

67.
Are You More or Less Frustrated Than Last Year?

When my father was in the hospital, I noticed his frustration was increasing.

He would complain a little bit more than normal.

In some ways, as my father aged, he became more patient. In other ways, he was quicker to allow his frustration to take over.

When I was a kid, he would yell at us to stop running in the house. When my sons were running around my parents' house last summer, he was much more tolerant. In fact, I could see that he enjoyed it.

But if he was caught in traffic, he would easily get annoyed, yelling at the person in front of him.

I think he was able to handle my sons running around the house because he felt grateful for them. He didn't feel the need to control their behavior, because that was my role. He could just enjoy them for who they were, even if they weren't behaving like perfect little boys.

He wasn't able to handle the traffic as well because he couldn't find appreciation in that situation.

If your frustration is increasing as you age, then you are allowing outside factors to determine your happiness.

If your frustration is decreasing as you age, then you are doing a better job of accepting the things outside of your control.

Practicing gratitude when we feel frustration coming on helps us to find growth in every difficult situation. The more we practice feeling appreciative, the easier it gets to let go of the things that frustrate us.

We can't be grateful and mad at the same time.

68.
Trade-Offs

It's not fair.

My younger son, Erik, gets the benefit of what I learned as a parent from my older son. He gets the more patient and less irritable me.

This morning, he was throwing an epic tantrum: toys flying through the air, tears streaming down his cheeks, little hands swinging slaps at my legs.

I calmly talked to him. Explained that I wasn't going to give him my scalding coffee no matter how much he screamed and thrashed.

My oldest would have gotten the "oh no you don't" treatment. I would have tried to talk to Gavin for thirty seconds, and if he didn't respond, well then, I would have picked him up and put him in time-out whether he liked it or not.

Erik gets the more compassionate treatment. I talk to him, explain why I'm making my decision, and sprinkle in a few calming words between flying toys and slaps.

I know that's how life goes. We all face different circumstances. Even now, I expect more from my older son because he is older. Sometimes I can be a little too tough, but it's hard to gauge this when I'm frustrated with his wandering attention.

I was the same way. An absent-minded professor who didn't follow other people's rules that well.

Gavin is lucky in many other ways. He got the more energetic dad when he was little.

We all get positives and negatives from a situation. It's what we focus on that matters.

I shouldn't worry about what I'm not giving each son.

If I focus on what I miss giving to my sons, then I'm focusing on the negative. Each one gets to see sides of me that the other doesn't. That's part of the adventure of raising children. I just try my best to appreciate what I can give them . . . and I hope they can appreciate it too.

69.
Watching Trees

I listened to the rustle of the leaves.

Not wanting to be anywhere else besides right here.

After just ten seconds, I could feel the voice in my head telling me to get back to work. I let that voice go like a puck sliding on an ice rink. It faded into the distance.

I brought my attention back to the moment. To the sounds of the leaves gently rubbing together.

It's hard to overstate the simple joy of nature . . . and the amazing joy of focusing on what matters right now.

70.
The Medicine
of Positive Projects

"I've been having trouble getting out of bed. I'm not sure what's wrong with me."

"Nothing's wrong with you," I told my friend. "I know when I felt that way, it was because I was depressed."

My friend looked at me and tried to smile, but he was in a difficult place.

I suffered through depression during my twenties and into my thirties. It was a rough time, but it taught me a lot about myself.

I remember locking myself in my apartment for days at a time and never coming out because I couldn't face anyone.

What got me through it was my family, my friends, and working on projects. One project in particular helped me stay grounded. I wrote a coffee table book called 92 Things to Do Besides Suicide. For each entry, I would take a picture of myself doing some sort of weird art project, like dipping cotton into Vaseline and sticking it to my face.

It made me focus on doing something besides wallowing in my own self-pity.

It was the best medicine for my internal woes. I feel so lucky that my father instilled in me the value of working on self-directed projects. This project encouraged me to laugh at myself when I needed to the most.

71.
Mosquito Net Lady

She sat on the bench, covered by a large piece of black netting.

I think she was protecting herself from mosquitoes.

Little kids were running right by her, stopping and whispering to each other.

One toddler pointed and asked, "Momma, what is she doing?"

At first glance, I didn't know what she was doing either. Then I realized she was meditating.

I appreciated her comfortableness in her own skin.

Then the old me started creeping in, and I mentally labeled her as weird. Why did she come to the park to do this when she could meditate at home?

Before I could go too far down this path, I brought myself back to my gratitude for her. I loved her boldness.

Then I thought about it some more. It's easy to meditate at home without any distractions, but someone who can meditate at a park can truly relax and focus on her breath in any situation. This woman was a gifted meditator.

I still don't think I would be comfortable enough to meditate in public with a big piece of black netting draped over me, but now I have a new bucket list item as a test for how comfortable I feel in my own skin. It might take me twenty years to get there, but at least I have something to aim for.

72.
Thinking About
All the Things I Have to Do

My alarm blared.

I opened my eyes.

It was pitch dark.

My first reaction was to worry.

I was facing a long list of things to deal with. I hadn't even had time to worry about all of them.

- » Redesigning a page on our website

- » An important meeting to discuss changes

- » My son's health

» My health

» Finding time to do yoga

The list went on.

Then I thought about how lucky I was to have this list.

A list like this can be very upsetting, or it can keep us engaged.

Two sides to the same situation.

If we pull away and try to detach ourselves from the things we have to do, we'll feel lost. If we're grateful for the difficult situations, we can learn from them.

My chronically upset stomach would be much worse if I hadn't been regularly breathing into my belly, which was helping me lower my stress levels at work. My son's illness reminded me that I was lucky to have a son who had been healthy 98 percent of his life, even though he was struggling with the flu right now.

My jaw relaxed.

These tasks and problems didn't exist last year. And next year will bring new ones.

I get to work on them one at a time. To do what I can, when I can, appreciating as much of the journey as humanly possible.

73.
Slowly Pulling Weeds

My fingers were down in the dirt, trying to get at the root of the weed.

I pulled little too fast, and the root broke. Most of it stayed in the dirt.

I looked up at the sky, sighed, and thought, Stupid weed.

I took a deep breath and tried another weed.

Gardening can be frustrating if I don't take my time.

I've come to realize that the weeds are trying to teach me a lesson. I can't rush the process, so I may as well enjoy it for what it is.

When I do take my time and I slowly wiggle the bottom of the weed in a circular motion so the root gradually comes up out of the dirt, it's oddly satisfying. Then on the next weed, I seem to forget this lesson and try to go a little faster, and the root stays in the ground again.

Then I try again, just a little slower than last time.

This time the root comes up out of the dirt, and I'm thankful.

74.
The Path

I hadn't seen my neighbor out in his front yard in a long time.

I was avoiding him on purpose.

A few weeks ago, there'd been no escape. I waved hi. My neighbor walked toward me, and I could feel myself cringe.

I didn't like that this was my first reaction.

This neighbor loves to complain about everything. Politics, weather, our neighbors, everything.

I used to complain a lot too. Just ask my wife. As I mentioned in an earlier story, I even complained about a Christmas present. I've gotten better, but sometimes I fall back into bad habits.

I wanted to bring more compassion to my relationship with my neighbor, but it was hard for me. It can be hard to feel gratitude for someone who complains all the time.

It doesn't mean it's not possible. Just that we have to take it on as a challenge.

Today, I decided to overwhelm my neighbor with gratitude.

He started with, "Man, it's too cold out here."

I countered with, "Yeah, don't you love it? It closes up all your pores."

He gave me an "Are you feeling ok?" look.

Then he complained about the upcoming mowing season. I told him that it's one of my favorite workouts.

He paused. He seemed unsure of how to handle my reframing of his negative comments.

Then he started to reverse his attitude.

He changed the subject to his upcoming fishing trip, and we had a lovely ten-minute conversation about his favorite bait to catch trout. I'm not big into fishing, but his excitement got me excited. I'd never seen him act this way.

Gratitude is one interesting tool.

75.
Misty

It was misting as I walked my son to school.

My mind was on an upcoming meeting that day.

My son giggled and shielded his eyes.

I kept walking. I didn't register his giggles. I was a little too focused on getting him in the school so I could get to my meeting.

After I dropped him off, his giggles sank in.

I missed an opportunity to giggle with him.

I could have taken ten seconds to join in with his giggling.

Focus is an underappreciated tool when trying to improve our capacity for gratitude. You can't appreciate simple things if your focus is distracted. Simple things like sitting on a soft-cushioned chair or walking in a warm-weather rain.

I was glad I'd noticed my lack of appreciation for my son's giggles. It reminded me of what was important to me.

I had missed so many opportunities for joy over the past few years, but if I focused on my failures, I'd go down a rabbit hole of worry that would only make me depressed. I didn't beat myself up for missing this opportunity to giggle with my son. I'd noticed my slip-up, and I could learn from it. Try to remember to be more present when the next opportunity to giggle with my son came along.

This thought made me realize something very important.

Earlier, I wrote about my discovery of "theming" a day, intentionally setting my focus. Now, I realized I didn't have to stick to one theme for each day. I could choose a theme for a specific situation, like walking my son to school. I could place my focus each morning on enjoying that time with my son, instead of letting my emotions and worries dictate my mindset.

Next time, I told myself, I will pounce on the moment and turn the giggles into belly laughs.

"I don't have to chase extraordinary moments to find happiness—it's right in front of me if I'm paying attention and practicing gratitude."

Brené Brown

76.
Screaming Kid

Erik, my two-year-old son, wanted to put on his own shoes.

I wanted to get to work on time.

Let the struggle begin.

Erik walked into the garage and got distracted by the broom. I asked him to sit down on a little bench, and it took some time before he listened to me.

I grabbed a pair of shoes as he moseyed on over to the bench. I got one shoe on, but then he said, "I do it! I do it!"

He took off the shoe I'd put on him. I sighed. He tried to put the shoe on. I snuck in some help and got both shoes on. Then he saw another pair of shoes he wanted to wear.

He said, "Off!"

I picked him up and said, "That's enough. It's time to get in the car."

He kicked his legs and screamed "NO!" at the top of his lungs.

I put him down. He was in full meltdown mode. He was crying and
flopping all over the dirty garage floor.

I grabbed him and put him back on the bench. I told him if he didn't
calm down, I wasn't going to help him put the new shoes on.

He looked at me and nodded to show me that he understood.

I took off his old shoes and put on the new ones. He seemed happy
for about two seconds. Then he wanted to put the other shoes back on
again.

At this point, I felt like I had only one option. I grabbed him and his
shoes and put him in his car seat. He cried the whole way to school.

The tears eased up as I parked the car. When I hugged him goodbye, he
was back to his usually happy self.

On my drive to work, I realized that he was teaching me a valuable
lesson. He was teaching me how to build the type of patience I'd always
wished I had. I was cool and calm through the whole process and never
let my emotions get too high or low while he was in full tantrum mode.

My son is giving me the gift of deep patience, one difficult situation at
a time.

77.
Attacking
Instead of Enjoying

My coworker was giving a big presentation to our peers.

He stumbled over the simple word "shareable."

He said "shareadle."

He laughed, corrected himself, and moved on.

I started attacking him in my head.

He didn't look people in the eye enough. He said "ah" and "um" too often. He wasn't as crisp as I would be up there, talking to people. My critique got more and more harsh as he continued.

As I mentally attacked him, I could feel tension building in my neck and face. I frowned with hatred.

Then he looked at me for reassurance. I smiled. It felt fake.

I didn't like my sour attitude toward him.

I felt awful. I was wishing for his failure. I wanted him to need me to save him, so I could be the hero. I was attacking him to make myself feel better.

I didn't feel better. I felt worse.

I stopped my internal critique and began listing things he was doing well. He made people laugh. He had a loose delivery that helped people feel at ease.

My tension released. I started breathing deeply again. I felt happy for him.

Even after all my gratitude practice, it's so easy to forget how gratitude can make any difficult situation just a little better. Sometimes it can be good to see other people's mistakes so we can learn from them, but it's not good to dwell on them and tear people down so we feel better.

I always seem to forget that helping other people succeed and grow is so much better for my happiness and health than hating on them in my own head. When we see people as allies instead of adversaries, we succeed and grow with them.

78.
Get off the Mental Hamster Wheel

The thought just wouldn't go away.

I was worried about the presentation that I had to give the next day.

I lay in bed, tossing and turning, thinking about what I was going to say.

I'm addicted to my worries.

They can make me feel alive and busy, but they also cause me a lot of pain.

A lot of pain.

I was frustrated with my inability to let go of my thoughts, and this compounded my overall frustration.

I had to get off this mental hamster wheel I was on.

So instead of feeding these thoughts and worrying myself even more, I thanked them for trying to help me.

Over the past several months, I've learned to step back and observe my feelings, enjoying what I can learn from them. I figured I could try the same thing with my thoughts and worries.

Instead of joining the worrying game and chasing the ball around, I decided to just become a spectator. I took a mental seat in the stands and watched. Not trying to control anything. Just watching.

I watched how my mind darted from a worry about an upcoming big meeting to a worry about my youngest son's ear infection.

When I was able to appreciate my thoughts, my frustration dissipated. It allowed me to relax and fall asleep.

When I awoke, I realized how far I'd come. Five years ago, I would have tossed and turned all night and had a really rough day. Now, I was a bit tired, but mostly felt fine.

I had a great day.

79.
New Angles

Last year, I pitched an idea at work and it bombed.

I wanted to change an important part of the website, and I was laughed out of the room.

I left with my tail between my legs.

Time passed, but I couldn't let the idea go. So I did some more research. I talked to people all over the organization and found out about a few more pain points. I mocked up some changes that reflected their ideas as well as my own.

A few months later, I pitched my idea with a new angle based on these pain points.

My colleagues loved it. The same people who had laughed me out of the room were now congratulating me for a good idea.

If my first idea hadn't been rejected, I wouldn't have worked to find a better solution that impressed the right people. Last year, I felt terrible after that failed presentation. I knew my idea was solid. I just needed a better way to explain it.

Setbacks are a part of life. It's how we deal with them—and even come to appreciate them—that helps us grow.

80.
Letting Go

I took a jog around a neighborhood park while my wife and kids stayed to play on the playground.

As I left my family to go on this jog, I felt a pang of regret.

I felt like I shouldn't be leaving them behind. I was worried that I was missing out on time with them.

As I jogged, I thought about work and the list of things that I needed to accomplish.

Then I thought about what I wanted to eat for dinner.

My jittery mind was having trouble enjoying the jog.

Before I went any further down this rabbit hole of worry, I thought, just let it go and enjoy where you're at.

Then, like usual, the worry came back. I worried about not spending enough time with my family.

Instead of giving in, I told myself to just let it go.

I had a nice fifteen seconds of enjoying myself, and then my brain went back to worrying about work.

I slowed down to a walk and focused on my breath. On appreciating the nature around me.

This went on for the rest of the jog. But as I continued, it got a little easier to let go and enjoy what I was doing for just a bit longer.

This is the practice of gratitude. Our minds wander off and we bring ourselves back to the beauty of the moment. Ask ourselves what is great about it. Then our minds wander, and again we bring back the gratitude.

It's a practice that every living person should try to improve on every single day. If you can master this skill, you'll be the master of your own happiness.

81.
Snapping

My son Gavin, who is seven, knows how to get on my last nerve.

He likes to get out of his chair during dinner and go sit on the couch, grab a toy from the toy box, lay on the floor, and do a hundred other things instead of eating.

One night, I asked him to sit down in his chair. He got up off the floor and just leaned against his chair with his feet on the floor. He's a pro at this game.

I raised my voice. "Gavin! Please sit down!"

He rolled his eyes.

I told him if I had to ask again, I was going to get very mad.

He scooted up in his chair. He refused to look at me for the next two minutes.

Later that night, I told my wife that I needed to do more meditation. She agreed. She thought I'd been a little too quick to get frustrated with Gavin lately.

My first reaction was to dismiss her feedback. Then I started to think about it, and she was right.

I was tougher on my older son, especially when I was feeling hungry. I needed to be a little fairer and a little more patient. I had to appreciate where his mindset was at when we ate dinner. He was in second grade, and he had to sit all day long. I remembered how I had all this pent-up energy at his age too.

I didn't want our relationship to be based on him acting out and me yelling at him.

So that night, I thought and prayed about being more compassionate to myself and my son as we both tried to help each other grow. I knew I was lucky to have a caring wife who gave me feedback so I could create a better relationship with my son.

The next night, I tried a new tactic. I tried to steer Gavin's focus back to his food and to the conversation at the table. I asked what his favorite food on his plate was. I asked what his favorite part of the day was. When he wandered off, I told him that he had ten seconds to enjoy wandering around the room, and then I would ask him to come sit back down.

It worked. The strategy of giving him ten more seconds encouraged him to come back to the table and stay longer than he had in the past few weeks.

82.
Give What You Can

I couldn't believe it.

I bought my coworker lunch last week, and he'd said he would pick up the tab this time. But he didn't. He owed me this lunch. I knew he remembered.

We paid our separate checks and the waitress placed the receipts on the table for us to sign. He didn't even acknowledge that he should have paid.

I was so mad!

I sat in silence, stewing in my anger. He kept asking me questions. I gave him short answers.

He finally asked me if everything was okay.

I blurted out, "I bought lunch last week. You said you would buy next time."

He apologized. He told me he and his wife had put themselves on a budget because of credit card debt. He offered to pay next time.

I felt bad.

Really bad.

I told him not to worry about it.

I'd been so worried about getting something in return for paying for his lunch last week. I'd been turning generosity into something negative, thinking of myself as doing something nice when I bought someone lunch, but expecting to get something out of it.

I shouldn't put these expectations on people. It's a bad habit.

If I buy lunch for someone, I should do it because I want to give to them. Giving just to give.

That's what generosity is actually about.

It's better to err on the side of generosity instead of keeping score of who owes me what. It just takes too much mental energy and pulls me away from feeling grateful for my time with my friends.

83.
Com'on!

"Com'on! Be in the moment!" I growled at myself.

I was at home, where I'd been finishing up a nice Sunday breakfast with pancakes, eggs, and a glorious cup of coffee. I hadn't been enjoying myself. I'd been thinking about how much I missed my father.

I'd caught myself and retreated to the bathroom to recalibrate my thoughts. That's when I growled at myself.

I hung my head. I thought I was doing better. But I just couldn't get the loss of my father out of my head today.

Of course, getting mad at myself wasn't helping.

I kept telling myself it was okay to be sad. But I wasn't dealing with the sadness very well.

A few weeks ago, I'd promised myself to meditate when I needed it.

Now was the time.

I did a short meditation.

My mind began to race as soon as I sat down and tried to focus on my breathing.

I remembered how my father had loved to hear stories about my two sons. I'd loved telling him those stories. He always laughed, especially when they were torturing me.

I smiled and let that thought drift away.

I came back to appreciating my breath.

Exhaled and took a deep breath in. I focused on savoring this simple action as much as I could.

I thought about how my father used to bring me with him to work.

He taught me to enjoy the details in my work.

I let that thought drift away.

I thanked my breath for helping me stay grounded.

I started to feel a lot better. All I'd needed was five minutes to recalibrate. I went back to my family to enjoy some time with them.

I'd tried short meditations to help me recalibrate in the past, and it had never worked. It was actually quite torturous. It usually turned into a big worry or complaint fest in my head.

I'd been missing a key ingredient.

Bringing gratitude to my meditation.

The present moment isn't beautiful until we're grateful for what it offers us. Even something as simple as a breath.

84.
My New Favorite Pen

I walked up to a vendor's table to see what she had to offer.

I talked with her for a few minutes. Just as I was about to walk away, she reached out and handed me a pen.

I thanked her and took it.

The pen was sticky around the grippy part, the part where you hold it. It annoyed me. I made a joke about how they didn't make pens like they used to.

The woman smiled and reached out a hand. "Give it here. I can fix it."

I handed it back, and she cleaned off the stickiness with a wet wipe.

She went the extra mile for me, and now I have a new favorite pen. Every time I use it, I think of this stranger's willingness to go above and beyond for me.

I'm grateful that this pen can help remind me to do the same for others.

85.
Not Moving
into the Turn Lane

I felt a burst of blood to my head.

"Get oooooveeeer," I whined.

I couldn't help myself. I raised my voice. "Com'on!"

I kept my language in check, but not my frustration.

My wife looked over at me, surprised.

I'd been driving home from the park in a perfectly good mood until I got stuck behind a slow driver. As we puttered along, he put his right turn signal on and never got in the turn lane.

Expectations are hard for me to deal with. I was expecting him to do what I would do in that situation, and he didn't.

It was such a small thing to get upset about. I let a perfectly good Sunday turn into something that made me angry, when clearly I should have just let it go and appreciated that I would soon be home—perhaps five seconds later than I wanted, but safe and healthy with my whole family.

I wish that I could thank that driver for showing me my current mindset—and for showing me that over the next few months, I need to continue to work on dealing with my anger.

86.
Angry at Inanimate Objects

I grabbed the ketchup and squeezed.

A few drops came out. I squeezed a little harder, and ketchup flooded over my burger.

"God!" I growled. "Always happens to me!"

I saw where my mood was heading and stopped. I decided to answer my unspoken question:

Why me?

Because I'm lucky to have access to ketchup.

Because I'm lucky enough to have a hot burger on my plate.

Because I can afford this nice table to sit at with my family.

Because I'm here to be able to breathe in the smell of this wonderful food.

Because no major disease has taken me down yet.

I picked up my burger, scraped the extra ketchup onto my plate, and dipped a sweet potato fry into it. The ketchup tasted amazing.

I'm one lucky man.

87.
Waking Up
with a Tight Jaw

My eyes popped open. It was the middle of the night.

My hair was drenched with sweat. I felt like someone had just punched me in the face. While I was sleeping, I had apparently clenched my teeth together so hard that my jaw was sore.

As I rubbed my jaw, I remembered my dream.

My father was in the hospital, and I couldn't find his room. I searched everywhere. It was dark, and no one would help me. Everyone was busy. I'd felt this panic coming on because I wouldn't be there to see him before he died.

I was still upset about my father's death.

Even when I felt all right in my waking life, my feelings were speaking to me in my dreams. Instead of pushing them aside, I listened. I was glad my jaw was sore, because it allowed me to remember my dream. It told me I still had some grieving to do before I could be at peace with my father passing away.

88.
Beauty in the Chair

My feet were sore.

My calves were burning.

I was enjoying this tired feeling. The hike we'd done that day had kicked my butt.

I saw a simple orange chair in the corner of my friend's apartment.

I reveled in the future feeling of sitting in that chair. Feeling the soft cushion on top of the hardwood.

I slowly walked over and started lowering myself into the chair. For a second, I thought about how much I was going to enjoy sitting down.

My butt sank into the cushion and I let out an "ahh."

So, so, good.

I would not have felt this way five years ago. My mind would have darted to my desire to eat or to what TV shows might be on.

Now, I knew I was going to enjoy the chair even before I sat in it. I took the time to prepare my mind for that simple joy.

I can sit in a chair without worrying about what will come next. It's taken so many hours of hard work for the ability to enjoy such a simple act.

It's been worth it!

Think of how many times each day we sit down in chairs. From the chair at the kitchen table to the driver's seat of a car to our office chairs to our meeting chairs and back to our office chairs and on to other meeting chairs . . . the list goes on. For many of us, it's probably around thirty times per day. Sometimes more. If we can make each one of those moments enjoyable, it's an easy way to improve our lives at work and at home.

89.
Up and Down

My friend Sam asked me what my favorite movie was, and my mind went blank.

"My favorite movie is . . . ah . . . well . . ."

I couldn't access my thoughts.

If someone asked me that now, I would say, "I have so many, but to pick a few, Ace Ventura, The Empire Strikes Back, WALL-E, Braveheart, and Old School." But trying to get the words out in that moment was impossible.

Later that day, I wanted to take my dog for a walk. Usually it's something I look forward to, but I just couldn't get myself motivated to take her out.

My mind had been slow lately, and my energy levels were down too.

I didn't feel sick, but I didn't have any pep that week.

Some weeks are just really easy to enjoy, while others are a bit of a struggle.

The ups and downs of life occur for us every single week. The more we appreciate the nuances of life, like peeling an orange or laughing at an awkward joke, the easier it gets to find the joys in the highs and lows.

90.
Someday You'll
Miss This

"I struggle with my computer so much. I wish I didn't have to change my password. Why does it do this?" my mom asked.

"One day you'll miss all this," I told her.

"I'm not good with all these changes," she said.

"I know. I'm not either."

"What? This is easy for you. Wait till you get to be my age."

"Wait until you're ninety," I told her. "You'll look back on this time and wish you could handle change as well as you do right now!"

She laughed and agreed.

Remember those carefree days as a kid?

Do you wish you could feel that young-kid magic again?

You'll look back on this moment, right now, and miss it. You'll miss those tough days at work, even the frustrating ones. You'll see how easy it would be to be happy, if you could just go back to that time with your current mindset.

It often takes a health scare to put our lives into perspective. I struggled through cancer, a terrible car crash, and a stomach virus that felt like it would never end.

Don't wait for a health scare to encourage you to feel grateful.

And if you have a health scare and are lucky enough to survive it, use it to help you change your life. It can be the leverage you need to start improving your ability to feel gratitude in every situation.

Something as simple as knee pain can show you how lucky you were when you could walk wherever you wanted without any pain at all.

When I'm struggling with work or a stubbed toe, I remember my father's last few days. He just wanted it all to be over. He knocked on death's door and entered.

I don't think he really utilized pain as a learning tool. He smashed wasps with his hands and waited for surgery until his hip was down to bone rubbing on bone. He usually just tried to tune out the pain. It seemed to work for the most part.

Even in his last few days, he never admitted to feeling any pain. I think he was so disconnected from his feelings that he fell into old habits of avoiding his pain.

I learned so much from his death. Here it was, almost a year later, and I was still uncovering things that I'd never understood before.

And as a result, I was making changes in my life. Simple changes, like playing with my kids instead of picking up my phone.

Every moment is a choice. We're either building better habits or strengthening weak ones. Sometimes it's the pain in life that really encourages us to take the paths that help us to become happier people.

91.
Thanking My Hair

I was slowly losing my hair.

It wasn't even close to the thick lustrous hair that I had in my twenties.

It was still hanging in there, but for my father it thinned a lot in his forties and fifties. I knew what I had to look forward to.

I pictured myself giving a presentation with a bald head. This thought made me sad. I felt sorry for myself. I noticed when I was washing my hair in the shower that it was falling out faster as my worries piled up.

I wondered why my hair was receding faster on one side than the other. Then I noticed that I would scratch the top of my head whenever I was stressed at work. I was rubbing away what was left of my hair.

Every time I looked in the mirror, I would get upset. I would clench my fists and growl at my thinning hair. I considered using special hair products that I knew didn't really help in an attempt to make it last longer.

I laugh at this memory now, even though it was just last year.

I now take a different approach. I touch the places where my hair is thinning, and I thank the hair that is left for hanging in there.

The simple habit of thanking my body for what I have left instead of mourning what I don't have anymore has been a powerful change.

92.
Don't Force It

I pulled into a parking spot at the grocery store.

My favorite Rolling Stones song was playing.

A hunched-over old woman was pushing her cart full of groceries to her car.

She was lucky.

I was lucky.

I turned off the engine, leaned back, and let the rest of the song play.

This moment was beautiful. There was no other moment like it.

I knew this, but I couldn't quite feel the joy I wanted to.

I knew I would only be this age, in this situation, with these people around me this one time. Of course I wanted to enjoy it.

But that's not always easy.

There are times I know that I need to be grateful for the moment, but it's hard. I want to feel more gratitude than I'm able to muster.

That's part of the beauty of gratitude. It ebbs and flows. It's a moving target that shouldn't be forced.

Feeling grateful doesn't need to be this intense wave that is constantly washing over us, making us feel lucky to be alive. There are many levels of feeling grateful. Some are strong and some are subtle.

Last week, I was sitting on the floor and playing with my son, and I found myself wanting to feel more grateful for the situation that I was in. I tried to force a deep sense of gratitude into the situation when it didn't need to be there.

I became a little frustrated with myself.

I got up and went to the bathroom, and I realized that I just needed to enjoy the moment for what it was. Not to force myself to feel a certain way. I was still enjoying my son; it just wasn't an intense joy that day.

I discovered it was okay to have that distant feeling of gratitude. To let go of my expectations and be present in a plain moment with my son, a moment when I was a little bit hungry and not feeling blissful.

I often feel like this when I'm shopping at the grocery store. I usually don't really want to be there, but I feel like I should be super grateful because I'm lucky enough to have all this great food at my fingertips. I can afford to buy whatever type of food my heart desires.

I am learning to be okay not needing to feel super grateful. To just watch my thoughts and my feelings as they come and go. I don't need to force intense gratitude.

The last notes of "You Can't Always Get What You Want" played on the radio.

I got out of my car and savored a new feeling of calm as I entered the store.

93.
I'm Glad
I Still Get Embarrassed

I was out at a Mediterranean restaurant with some friends. Everyone was joking and laughing.

I made a joke about not liking yogurt because I slipped on it and hit my head as a kid.

My friends went silent, and I blushed.

My first reaction was to gloss over it. I tried to change the subject, but they weren't having it. They started making fun of my bad joke.

I laughed at my lameness, and they laughed too.

We laughed together.

I can't win them all.

After getting over trying to ignore my embarrassment, I soaked it in. I reveled in it. The older we get, the less embarrassed we get when we do something like make a bad joke. It's a feeling we probably won't feel as often in the future, so we may as well try to appreciate it when it happens.

94.
Spewing Water

After treating my washing machine drainpipes with bacteria-eating enzymes, I went to bed.

The next day, my wife started a load of laundry. I'd forgotten to put the drain hose back into the drain opening behind the washing machine. I was in the kitchen when I heard it gushing out.

I ran to the washing machine, saw the water pouring out of the hose, and put it back into the drain.

No swearing.

No spewing anger.

No frustration.

I laughed at my forgetfulness and wrote myself a note not to forget that again.

95.
The Downhill Battle

We finished up a big website change.

My team was ecstatic. As we left the meeting, someone said, "Hey, I have an idea for the next project."

Then we all began to discuss our ideas as we went back to our desks.

I usually work hard on a project but don't take time to enjoy it once I've finished. I don't soak in the moment. I'm already moving onto the next thing.

It's why I love riding my bike. I pedal up a hill, and when I'm at the top, I have the wind to help me stay in the moment as I glide down. It's a constant positive reminder of the hard work I did to pedal up the hill.

It's important that we take time to enjoy our hard work.

Sometimes I forget to reflect after a tough day or a tough project, and I don't sleep as well. It's not until the next day that I realize that reflection helps me settle down and enjoy what I've accomplished.

The older I get, the more time I take to reflect throughout the day. It can be as simple as a bathroom break or a quick break to get a glass of water. I think through everything, and then I jot down a few quick notes to help me remember, process, and appreciate as much of the moment as possible.

Keeping a gratitude journal has done wonders for my happiness. It's a simple and powerful tool that I'd like to share with you.

Ask yourself:

> » How does it feel to finish the project?
>
> » What was the best part of the project?
>
> » Who was a big help? (Can I go and thank them right now?)
>
> » What did I learn from the project?
>
> » What was most interesting about the project?

These kinds of questions can help us to think through everything and figure out what worked well and what didn't. When we take the time to pause and reflect after each project, we allow space for gratitude to soak in.

96.
The Bathroom Incident

Shooting pains raced through my stomach.

I'd just pulled into the grocery store parking lot with my two young sons. It felt like my insides were about to explode. My lunch wasn't sitting well. I'd been eating too much at each meal again. The way I was dealing with my stress was catching up with me.

There was no time for me to drive back home. We rushed inside. My sons wanted to go in opposite directions, so I picked both of them up and ran into the bathroom. There was no time to explain. Erik was crying and Gavin wouldn't stop asking questions.

"Why are we in here? . . . Where are we going? . . . I don't want to go to the bathroom—I want to get a free sample and check out the toy aisle."

The funny thing is, even in that tough situation, I was grateful for the bathroom. I felt lucky because the bathroom stall was unoccupied. Erik tried crawling underneath the stall, and luckily it was too low for him, so he had to stay in the bathroom stall with me. I felt grateful for the designer who made these stalls.

Before I started this gratitude journey, I would've been very frustrated. My anger would have boiled over, and I probably would have snapped at my kids, even though the situation wasn't their fault. This time I just rolled with it.

Every time we're in a frustrating situation, we have a chance to reframe it. Even tough situations have a positive aspect to them. We can ask ourselves, "How can I find the tiny little positive in this situation?"

It's not always easy—it certainly wasn't easy when my insides felt like they were going to explode, but after it was all over, I was able to see all the small gifts that added up. The store that allowed me the free use of the bathroom. The powerful air conditioning that cooled me off as soon as we got inside. The fact that that I was strong enough to pick up my two-year-old and run with both kids into the store. How well they both handled the situation.

I had a lot to be thankful for.

97.
Knowing What I Need

I lay flat on the ground, just following my breath in and out.

A soft tingle started in my head and rippled down to my toes.

I know I need meditation. It helps me relax and brings good ideas to light.

I'd been forgetting this.

Again.

Getting something through my thick head and building a good habit is always a struggle.

I sighed.

After taking a few days off, I'd just practiced yoga and done five minutes of meditation. I felt great. My body kept this subtle, gentle tingle going, and I thought of a good idea for a story for my book.

I know meditation is good for me, but I don't do it as often as I should.

You probably know how hard it is to maintain a good habit. It takes a long time to make it a part of your routine.

Try to think of the last time you resisted a sweet treat at a birthday party or at work. I know I give in more often than I should. It's not that I need the extra calories. It's just hard to say no because of the social aspect and the sugary boost of a slice of cake.

It's also hard to say yes to things that are good for us, but aren't a part of our routine.

By starting small, I've been able to build habits like yoga and meditation into my routine.

I usually trick myself into doing yoga at night by telling myself I'm only going to do it for five minutes.

I can do anything for five minutes.

Then once I'm a few minutes in, the yoga session feels so good I know that I'll end up doing more like fifteen or twenty minutes and adding a short five-minute meditation at the end. It's truly the best way for me to spend my time at night.

98.
I Shouldn't Enjoy This

My butt was feeling very irritated.

An intense burn.

Several different ideas popped in my head to fix the issue, but the one that made the most sense was rubbing lotion on my butt.

I got out of the shower, squirted some lotion on my hand and rubbed it on my butt. I felt very awkward, scared someone might open the door and laugh at me.

I'm a forty-year-old man and high school insecurities still find a way to creep into my life.

After the first five seconds, I stopped feeling uneasy and just relaxed and actually enjoyed the process. It was exactly what I needed. It felt weird to be enjoying this moment as much as I was. Part of me just wanted to get the process over with, while the other part of me wanted to enjoy the relief the lotion provided.

It didn't cure my pain, but it reduced it by at least 80 percent. I've been practicing being more present in the actions that I take, appreciating the details within each sensation.

After I relaxed and stopped worrying about how somebody else might view the situation, I just let it be enjoyable.

We often worry about how somebody else might view the things we do. It's important that we let this go and not let other people's perceptions affect how we go about our lives. If we can do this, we'll go a long way toward living the lives we desire.

It starts with small things like embracing an awkward situation as best as we can without wanting to rush through it.

99.
This Moment,
Not the Next One

I was doing one of my favorite things in the whole world.

Reading a book to my son.

I felt this subtle discontent. I was reading faster than I'd planned to. I was even skipping pages.

I wanted to watch the game on TV. It was the playoffs and my favorite team was playing.

Of course, I knew that when I looked back in ten years, I wasn't going to remember if my team had won, but I would remember the moments I got to read to my son. I knew this because I didn't remember how many games my team won last year, but I did remember my son sitting in my lap or lying next to me and touching the hairs on my arm as I read.

This was my time to practice enjoying the moment instead of wanting to be in the next one.

So I slowed down, kissed my son on the head, and kept reading.

I soaked in the moment.

And guess what?

The game was still on after I was done reading.

100.
Mindset Tools

I once asked my friend Rob, "If you could give me one compliment, what would it be?"

I said it as a joke. I told him he didn't have to answer.

He said, "You always know the right thing to say."

I was stunned. I wasn't expecting one of the best compliments I've ever received.

I'm lucky to have such a good friend. I'm lucky to have a gratitude toolbox to go to anytime I need a boost. At the end of this book, you can see the mindset tools that I use myself (and offer to my clients).

We all go through our own issues. That's why having a gratitude toolbox is so important. One of my favorite tools is utilizing a friend's point of view. When you ask a positively phrased question to a good friend, you'll get a boost.

Try one of these questions:

> » What is my greatest strength?
>
> » What historical figure do I most remind you of?
>
> » Why do you enjoy hanging out with me?
>
> » What is your favorite memory about our relationship?
>
> » How do I challenge you to be a better person?

You have an opportunity to enjoy every situation you are in if you are willing to be creative and try hard to make the experience better. Next time you are stuck in a rut, try leaning on one of your good friends to give you a boost. Send me a message through BringGratitude.com and let me know how it works. I would love to see if this idea helps you.

"Your attitude is like a box of crayons that color your world. Constantly color your picture gray, and your picture will always be bleak. Try adding some bright colors to the picture by including humor, and your picture begins to lighten up."

Allen Klein

101.
Reality Show

The woman looked at me, crossed her eyes, and laughed like a madwoman.

I was caught off guard.

She loved my shocked expression.

She winked and walked away.

I was standing at the counter at my local coffee shop. She'd been in front of me. She'd ordered this crazy-detailed drink with coconut milk and dash of almond milk, chocolate whipped cream, and a dash of vanilla.

I'd said, "Now that is a woman that knows what she wants."

Then she laughed really loud. It surprised me.

I thought about her all day.

She made my day interesting.

I felt like I was on a reality show. As if the camera was on me, waiting to capture my expression after this woman's crazy laugh.

That crazy lady opened up a hidden place of gratitude inside of me.

In a way, everyone is living in their own reality show. We each see life from a single perspective, and the right comment at the right moment can create an amazing cascade of reactions. Every interaction is a chance to be surprised. We can choose to interact and go deeper, or we can hide ourselves away.

More and more, I'm choosing to go deeper—and each time I do, my appreciation grows for the crazy and wonderful people around me.

102.
The Rabbit Hole

I had been in a rut for a few days.

A low mental fog was weighing me down.

I leaned back in my chair, then sat up again as I heard the new-email alert from my work computer.

I read the email. My boss wanted a specific file for his boss.

My stress level picked up a notch.

As I looked all over my computer and searched our network for the file, I started to freak out. I couldn't find it. Acute anxiety stabbed my stomach. My hands were sweating, and I clenched my fists. The file wasn't in any of the folders where I would normally save it.

If I didn't find the file, it would look like I was disorganized. My boss would think I was an idiot. How could I ever expect to get a promotion? I didn't have time to recreate the file.

How quickly I can go down a rabbit hole of dark thoughts.

I was falling back into old bad habits. The negative thoughts happened so fast. I was going down the rabbit hole, but something inside my brain made me stop.

Instead of feeding into these feelings and letting them get me more upset, I watched them and tried to appreciate the different experiences that these feelings brought me. The stabbing pain in my stomach was interesting. My stress had never felt like that before. I also had a quick idea of avoiding the whole situation. I chuckled at this thought. I knew that wouldn't help.

I took two deep breaths. I then realized that my coworker might have the file.

I walked over to my coworker and asked him if he had the file. He looked in a few different folders and within a few minutes . . .

He found it!

He saved my butt.

He dropped the file in my network folder.

I sent it to my boss.

Relieved.

This internal freak-out opened up my appreciation.

I was glad I stayed calm when talking to my coworker. No freaking out. I focused on being clear about what I was looking for and why I needed it.

My freak-outs always come when I least expect them. That's why it's so important for me to watch how I react instead of letting myself go down a rabbit hole of negativity. The deeper I've gone into gratitude, the more I'm starting to realize that thoughts are just that: thoughts. They don't have control over me.

It's like I'm watching someone else. I just get to see it from my own eyes. My own reality TV show. Just a really interesting show that is constantly teaching me new things about myself.

This was an amazing realization that took a lot of work to understand.

I care deeply for this character that is me, but when I'm having a rough time, I can always turn off the show by coming back to gratitude. This resets my mindset and allows me to stop taking myself too seriously.

Nothing in my life is worth letting my anxiety get the best of me. Nothing is worth stressing myself out. I want to live happy and healthy until I'm a hundred. Every moment is just something to learn from and appreciate.

The trick is not letting what is happening, good or bad, affect my knowledge of how lucky I am to be living in this moment.

103.
Listening to My Body

I thought I'd solved my stomach issues when I gave up eating avocados.

I'd found out I was allergic to them. They made me dizzy and nauseous.

I'd had issues with my stomach for most of my life. I'd given up a lot of foods: dairy, red meat, grains, sugar, and now avocados. But at least, I thought, the problem would finally be solved.

I should've known better.

One morning, months after giving up avocados, I woke up feeling bloated, with severe stomach pain. It felt like a toddler had been practicing karate chops to my stomach all night long.

My stomach is my Achilles heel. It's much better than it was when I was in my twenties, but it's still annoying.

I watch other people eating barbecue ribs, fast food, and ice cream, and I think to myself, Man, I wish I could have a bowl of ice cream too. It's just not in the cards for me. I'm slowly coming to appreciate this fact.

Instead of letting jealousy take over, I've learned to be grateful for the healthy parts of my body, like my legs, my back, and my mind. I still have an amazing life filled with great projects, hugs from my kids, kisses from my wife, and walks with my dog.

Everyone has something they are currently struggling with.

Everyone.

My brother has back issues and high blood pressure. I have a friend who has really bad breath. Another friend who has terrible migraines. Another friend who struggles with depression. Another friend with a bad knee. Another friend who has money issues. I have quite a few friends with relationship problems.

The list goes on. I don't have a single friend who doesn't struggle with something.

We all struggle with some kind of physical or emotional pain. We all have an Achilles heel.

If you can accept this and allow it to be your teacher, then you'll notice a lot of internal growth. You will learn to turn your weakness into a strength.

I quit drinking alcohol, and I gave up many foods I loved. My father would say, "Kill me now if I have to give up those things."

I have more energy now than I've had in the last ten years. I'm actually happier without them.

I'll still have a donut now and again, but only maybe once or twice a month. I've changed my routine to include better breathing, more yoga, more meditation, more writing, more walking, more playing on the floor with my kids, more savoring the moments that I'm in on a daily basis.

My stomach issues have forced me to be a better person. That's only happened because I listen to my body and think of my stomach as a partner in my health, showing me how I can improve my life.

I'm glad I have a sensitive stomach. It's been one of the greatest teachers I've ever had.

104.
Silence

I sent a text to see if a few of my friends wanted to hang out after work.

Silence.

My wife had taken the kids out to eat with a friend, and I was on my own. I'd thought about just getting takeout and watching a movie, but I thought it would be more fun to hang out with a small group.

Putting ourselves out there and feeling the rejection of silence is never easy.

If a bunch of my friends had said, "Sorry, I can't do it," then I would've understood, but the silence hurt so much more. It was a blow to my ego. I felt like I was back in high school, afraid to ask anyone to hang out.

I knew it was short notice, but I thought somebody would want to hang out and grab a bite to eat.

Later that night, I had a dream where all my coworkers were laughing at my "do you want to hang out?" text while I hid behind a wall. When I woke up, I felt very insecure.

There was this brief moment when I felt like not going into work, but then I realized my feelings were just feelings, and having a feeling doesn't make it true.

Just because my friends didn't text me back didn't mean that they didn't like me. I began to list all the great aspects of my friends. From Rob's sense of humor to DJ's wit. These people bring so much joy into my life. I was lucky to have them as friends, even though they didn't text me back.

So I went into work and when I saw a friend of mine, the first thing he said was, "Do you want to go grab lunch? Sorry I wasn't available yesterday."

I appreciated him asking me to lunch and letting me know he was sorry. It eased my social anxiety.

I actually ended up having a great day.

We're human. We want to be liked by people. This isn't a bad thing, but if we let it overwhelm us, it can take us into a dark place. The practice of letting our feelings go and being grateful for what each moment has to offer is such a blessing.

105.
The Bounce Back

A guy cut me off in traffic. I hit my brakes and got stuck at a red light; he made it through. For a few seconds, I felt this deep anger rise up.

I noticed it and thanked it.

I calmed down immediately. That was weird. I'd never calmed down that fast before.

My anger showed me that I almost let one crazy driver wreck my day.

I struggled with seeing the positive in a situation for most of my life. It's one of the most important skills that happy people use. They bounce back quickly, not because they are happy, but because they find a way to appreciate what each moment offers them.

When you can find gratitude in a tough situation, you spark your ability to reframe and learn from the situation. It's this practice that builds mental strength.

I'm still a little surprised that I thanked my anger. For years, I've thought of my anger as an enemy. How naïve I've been.

Even anger can be something to appreciate and learn from.

106.
Patterns

My dog had just pooped on my neighbor's lawn.

I reached down for the doggie-bag dispenser on the leash, and it was empty!

Nooooooo!

My first thought was, Why me?

Then I thought about how I could use this as an opportunity. I saw a neighbor a couple houses down. I walked over and asked her for a plastic bag. She was happy to give me one. I embraced the moment as a chance to get to know one of my neighbors better. I asked her about her weekend plans. She said she was going to a kite festival.

I looked it up on my phone, and it looked like a lot of fun. I decided to take my boys.

We went and had a great time.

Maintaining a practice of conscious gratitude and awareness has really helped me. Now that it's been over a year, I'm seeing a lot of patterns emerge.

You've probably seen some patterns in this book as well. The same topics and tactics arising at different times, in different ways.

Things like:

» Becoming a watcher of your thoughts and feelings

» Practicing letting go of your anger and bringing your attention back to all the good things in your life

» Finding the positive in a difficult situation just by adjusting your mindset (reframing)

» Focusing on the beauty all around you instead of complaining about what is upsetting you

» Finding ways to thank the moment you are in, in order to bring more joy into your life

Do you see other patterns in this book?

Do you see patterns in your life?

Do you get mad every time you are in traffic? Do you get frustrated with the same people week after week?

You can continue to follow your current patterns, or you can choose to look for things to learn from and appreciate about every person or situation.

That's why reframing your situation is so important. If you only take away one tool after you stop reading this book and go about your life, that's the one I want to pass on.

Next time your coworker makes you mad, use it as an opportunity to observe your emotional patterns without feeding into these emotions. Notice your feelings, let them go, and focus on what you appreciate about your current situation.

Next time you are stuck in traffic, use it as an opportunity to have fun in the situation instead of wanting it to be different.

Next time your dog poops in your neighbor's lawn and you don't have a plastic bag, use it as an opportunity.

107.
Why I Struggle
with the Holidays

I was listening to a playlist on my phone. A song from the Grinch Christmas special came on. It was the end of summer, and I was already starting to look forward to Christmas.

Then all of a sudden, I got sad.

It was weird.

My emotions were telling me something my mind couldn't process.

Instead of ignoring this feeling, I decided to take the dog for a walk and think about it a bit.

I knew I'd miss my father not being around.

I started thinking about the pressure of finding the right present for everyone on my list.

I've come to realize that I struggle with the holidays because I expect so much. I want the holidays to be perfect for my family.

As I've become aware of these expectations, I've practiced noticing them when they arise. Letting go of the idea of a "perfect" experience.

It will take some practice, but I would like to bring more gratitude to the coming holiday season. Whether I end up in an awkward conversation with a family member or accidentally overcook the stuffing, it can be a learning situation that will help me grow.

108.
The Law of Gratitude

I stood at the train station, waiting patiently. An old man sat on the bench, his cane between his knees. He was leaning his chin on the top of his cane, staring off into space.

A gentle breeze blew by and a white napkin came with it.

I felt so lucky to be a part of this simple moment.

I felt like I was in a living Van Gogh painting.

I felt full of gratitude.

The law of gratitude is strong. Gratitude makes simple things amazing.

Over the past year, I've noticed that as I bring more gratitude to work, more people want to be around me. They're stopping by my desk to chat. I'm attracting positivity back to me.

I thought that focusing on gratitude for a whole year would help me deal with my father's death, but I didn't expect the perk of being more of a magnet for positive and energizing people. The funny thing is, I'm not sure if I'm just now attracting these people into my life, or if they have always been there, but now I'm more grateful for their friendship.

109.
Thank You

I'm very grateful for you. Your attention. Your time in processing these stories. I can't thank you enough.

I'm grateful for my father's encouragement to keep at my writing to help others. His wisdom lives on through this book.

I'm grateful for my editor Katherine Miller, who has helped me take this book to the next level.

I'm grateful for inspiration from:

Walter Staib (my father)

Elsa Staib (my mother)

Nikki Staib

Alex Kjerulf

Traci Fenton

Tony Hsieh

Lori Deschene

Marc Chernoff

Angel Chernoff

Mike Vardy

Chris Guillebeau

Gary Vaynerchuk

Chris Brogan

Jonathan Fields

Pam Slim

Charlie Gilkey

Leo Babauta

Jeff Goins

Courtney Carver

Joshua Becker

J.D. Roth

Rob Miller

Albert Rodriguez

Their wisdom and great writing paved the way for me. Without them, I would never have written this book.

I'm grateful that you made it all the way through this book. That tells me you are not only open to the idea of feeling grateful—you are also open to the idea of using gratitude for growth.

Like anything, you can practice gratitude and get decent at it, or you can really dig down and allow it to change how you think and feel.

I'm a big proponent of the deep dive. I think it's easy to trick ourselves into believing that we've done everything we can do to be more grateful. That's the moment when just a little more hard work can open up a whole new world to us.

I've still got a long way to go. I still have daily struggles, like the time last week when I yelled at my dog for barking while my two-year-old was sleeping. But I still look forward to every step of my future because of how lucky I feel to be experiencing my life. Even my angry moments are learning opportunities, and they don't last as long as they used to. I come back to gratitude and the anger drips off of me.

My challenge to you is to pick one of the stories in this book and apply the example to your life. I suggest starting with #56. Thank everything and everyone in your mind for a whole day. It's hard, and you'll lose focus, but it's an amazing exercise that will give you a glimpse into the power of gratitude.

Whatever exercise you choose to apply to your life, try it for just one week. Give yourself that. And watch what happens.

Gratitude Toolbox

Throughout this book, I've tried to pick up gratitude and look at it from every angle possible. The deeper you delve into a particular subject, I find, the more likely it will stick with you. I've tried to be honest about my struggles as well as the good times, in the hope that perhaps you can learn from my mistakes. That you can stand on my shoulders and reach a little higher than me.

A few days ago, I had a difficult conversation with a friend about gratitude.

I was gushing with joy about how gratitude changed my life.

He didn't see it that way.

He's a bit of an Eeyore, usually focusing on the negative. "Gratitude is a waste of time," he said. "Why would I share gratitude with anyone? It just gets in the way of my focus. People shouldn't need validation. It's a weakness."

I'm glad he brought me down from my perch on cloud nine, because it was a good reminder that gratitude is not the secret to happiness. It's just one tool in a cabinet of tools that make for a happy and healthy person.

The only way gratitude will improve anyone's life is if that person admits that they need it and makes it a priority.

For most of his life, my father was afraid to tell me he loved me. I knew he loved me. He showed me through his actions, through his affection and the time he spent with me, through the way he imparted wisdom when he felt it was appropriate.

I think a big reason I was so sad when he died was that in the end, he finally showed me how much he appreciated me with his words.

He loved me, but I waited so long to hear those words you always want to hear from your father.

I love you.

When he finally said them to me, they were what I needed when I really needed it the most.

I think people who see gratitude as a waste of time fail to see the larger point. Gratitude is a stepping stone for happiness. We can use it as inspiration to help ourselves grow.

If you are always wishing for more (whether that's money, time, or friends), you'll never be happy. No matter how much you have, you can always want more. Many rich people are unhappy.

Yes, there are unhappy billionaires. They commit suicide, deal with addictions, or fly into a rage when they get stuck in traffic jams.

There are poor people who are unhappy, too.

But those people who feel grateful for what they have live blessed lives.

It's not about settling. It's about appreciating the challenge that life has put before you.

Gratitude inspires resilience.

Let's review some of the most important tools from this book. I suggest turning one of these into a habit by practicing it every single day for thirty days.

Get the 5 Tools one page guide that you can print out at BringGratitude.com/tools so you can build the gratitude habit.

Keep a gratitude journal

Write down three things that you are grateful for at the end of each day. Remember to be as detailed as you can. The more detail you record, the more this practice will stick with you. If you are busy or tired, just keep it simple, but when you do have time to write down some details, try it.

The key here is to do this every single day for thirty days. If you can do it for a whole year, even better.

Stories to review:

19 – I'm Lucky Because . . .

95 – The Downhill Battle

109 – Thank You

Reframe a tough situation

Whenever you are dealing with a difficult situation like being stuck in traffic, you can frame it as a waste of time or you can frame it as a chance to do something fun. Like having a dance party in your car.

Stories to review:

48 – Labels

96 – The Bathroom Incident

105 – The Bounce Back

Show gratitude

One of the greatest gifts you can give someone is acknowledging their hard work. When they see that you notice how hard they've worked, they light up inside. This is a gift that you can give at work and at home. Thank your kids for helping you empty the dishwasher. Explain why they are doing such a good job. Thank your coworkers every time they impress you. They'll want to work on more projects with you.

Make it your mission to thank everything that you interact with for one day. It's not an easy task, but as you do it, you'll notice you are setting yourself up for success and happiness all day long.

Stories to review:

49 – Pouring Hot Water into My Tea Mug

54 – Thank Everything

56 – The Power of Gratitude

Theme small events

Suppose you have an early flight tomorrow to get to a business meeting. Let's say take-off is 6:00 a.m., which means you have to be up by 3:00 a.m.

You can worry about how early you have to get up and how tired you'll be, or you can choose another theme. You can theme the morning.

The theme for that small part of your day could be:

"Extra-special cup of coffee" morning – Take the time to savor every sip of your cup of coffee just a bit more than you did yesterday.

"Self-evolved people at the airport" morning – See how many positive people you can count at the airport. (You can count the happy and chirpy people.)

"Greet a lot of people" morning – See how many people you can say hello to. Ask how their mornings are going.

"Big energy meeting" morning – Try to bring as much energy as you can to the meeting by focusing on your body language and tone of voice.

Choose themes that help you focus on the potential positive aspect of the upcoming event. By looking for the positives in each situation, you'll create a positive domino effect that will ripple through the rest of your day.

Stories to review:

These four gratitude tools are very powerful. They've done wonders for my happiness and relationships. I look forward to hearing about how they help you.

* * *

Remember that as you show more gratitude, you'll start to feel like this is the new normal. The boost of energy and happiness that gratitude gives you will eventually dissipate. Psychologists refer to this as the "hedonic treadmill." The idea is that you run really hard to get something, and the thing you get feels good, but then you adapt to it and you have to run harder to get more of this thing. Gratitude works the same way. And once you stop getting an emotional boost from gratitude, it's easy to let it fall off your radar.

It can be especially hard to be grateful when you're having a rough day. When my father was in the hospital, I didn't feel like being grateful. I tried, but I kept snapping back to a negative mindset. I had to do a little trick.

This last item for your toolbox comes from researcher Tom Gilovich, a professor of psychology at Cornell University. In "Why Is My Life So Hard?" on the Freakonomics Radio podcast, he suggests you ask yourself:

"What are the ways in which I'm boosted along, the invisible things that make my life easier?"

Your answers could help you see some of the small things you tend to take for granted. The fact that the toilet paper roll is full and you don't need to shuffle to the cabinet for a new roll (or worse yet, realize you forgot to restock it!). The fact that your car starts in the morning.

One of my favorite approaches to this is paying attention to the jobs people do that generally go unnoticed. I try to thank the people who work in convenience stores, restaurants, and cafeterias, because without them I wouldn't be able to eat when I'm hungry.

Falling into negative thinking—blaming others for not replacing the toilet roll, or bemoaning our hard lot in life—is a trap. It's easy to summon unpleasant emotions. We are hard-wired to seek safety. The more we accumulate, the safer we think we will feel. Greed and envy grow out of this deep-rooted survival instinct.

We worry that if we feel grateful, we'll get complacent and stop striving for more.

But once we're in a scarcity mindset, it doesn't matter how much we have. Look at the wealthy people who have ten million in assets, but want twenty million. If they get twenty million, they'll want fifty million. They will never feel like they have enough.

To get to a point where we can appreciate what we have—not what other people have—we have to start small. We have to bring gratitude to the little things in our lives.

Where can you bring more gratitude into your life?

If you want to find out, try using one of these gratitude tools for the next thirty days. It usually takes about thirty days to build a habit. I'm a little thickheaded, so it took about ninety days for it to really work for me, but it worked well. Once you build this habit, you will notice improvements in your relationships, your career, and your health.

You can visit me at BringGratitude.com/tools to get the 5 Tools one page guide that will help you increase your productivity by 31%. Just message me at karl@bringgratitude.com and let me know if you have any questions at all. I'll be happy to help.

31 Percent
More Productive
Coaching, Speaking, and Courses

We help leaders and companies tap into the power of gratitude. In his book Why We Do What We Do, Edward Deci demonstrates that if you can bring more positivity into your workplace, you'll increase your team's productivity by 31 percent.[4] That's a big improvement. The key is implementing systems that are specifically tailored to your organization. That's where we can help.

If you are interested, just reach out to us at BringGratitude.com.

Great Gratitude Quotes

I've found a good quote can help me see my current situation from a whole new angle. It's the inspiration that I need to do great work. Here are some of my favorites:

"Gratitude unlocks the fullness of life. It turns what we have into enough, and more. It turns denial into acceptance, chaos to order, confusion to clarity. It can turn a meal into a feast, a house into a home, a stranger into a friend." - Melody Beattie

"Life experience is what defines our character, even if it means getting your heart broken or being lied to. You know, you need the downs to appreciate the ups. Going on the adventure or taking that risk is important." - Nev Schulman

"Gratitude is the healthiest of all human emotions. The more you express gratitude for what you have, the more likely you will have even more to express gratitude for." - Zig Ziglar

"'Did I win? Did I lose? Those are the wrong questions. The correct question is: Did I make my best effort?' If so, he says, 'You may be outscored but you will never lose.'" - Carol S. Dweck, quoting UCLA Coach John Wooden

"I don't have to chase extraordinary moments to find happiness— it's right in front of me if I'm paying attention and practicing gratitude." - Brené Brown

"Beauty is when you can appreciate yourself. When you love yourself, that's when you're most beautiful." - Zoe Kravitz

"I do believe that if you haven't learnt about sadness, you cannot appreciate happiness." - Nana Mouskouri

"My dad encouraged us to fail. Growing up, he would ask us what we failed at that week. If we didn't have something, he would be disappointed. It changed my mindset at an early age that failure is not the outcome, failure is not trying. Don't be afraid to fail." - Sara Blakely

"Give yourself a gift of five minutes of contemplation in awe of everything you see around you. Go outside and turn your attention to the many miracles around you. This five-minute-a-day regimen of appreciation and gratitude will help you to focus your life in awe." - Wayne Dyer

"Gratitude is the inward feeling of kindness received. Thankfulness is the natural impulse to express that feeling. Thanksgiving is the following of that impulse." - Henry Van Dyke

"Thank you" is one of the most powerful combinations of words in any language. When used well, it can change lives.

Use these next few pages as a chance to start your gratitude journal.

List three things you are grateful for right now. Explain why for each one.

1.

2.

3.

List three ways in which you're boosted along: the invisible things that make your life easier. Explain why for each one.

1.

2.

3.

List three things you are grateful for right now. Explain why for each one.

1.

2.

3.

List three ways in which you're boosted along: the invisible things that make your life easier. Explain why for each one.

1.

2.

3.

Theme Your Day
Around Gratitude

Day of the Week   Theme

Monday: (Ex. Today I will enjoy the weird personalities of all my
coworkers.)

Tuesday:

Wednesday:

Thursday:

Friday:

Saturday:

Sunday:

Because when you set your intention for the day it makes it easier to stay grateful even when you are having a tough day.

Notes

1. Seligman, M.E.P., T.A. Steen, N. Park, and C. Peterson. 2005. "Positive Psychology Progress: Empirical Validation of Interventions." American Psychologist 60, no. 5 (July/August): 410–421.

2. Burton, Chad, and Laura King. 2004. "The Health Benefits of Writing About Intensely Positive Experiences." Journal of Research in Personality 38, no. 2 (March/April): 150–163.

3. Wiseman, R. 2003. "The Luck Factor." The Skeptical Inquirer 27, no. 3 (May/June): 1–5.

4. Deci, E. L. 1996. Why We Do What We Do. New York: Penguin.

Made in the USA
Columbia, SC
17 November 2020

24794400R00178